ANATOMY OF SUICIDE

ANATOMY OF SUICIDE

Editor
V.C. Pandey

ISHA BOOKS
DELHI-110 033

Anatomy of Suicide

Rs. 880

ISBN: 81-8205-147-9

Published in 2005 in India by
Isha Books, D-43, Prithviraj Road,
Adarsh Nagar, Delhi-110 033

Laser Typesetting at : Shree Vaishnavi Creations, Delhi
Printed at : Chawla Offset Press, Delhi

Contents

Preface

Suicide is the action of killing oneself intentionally. It is a multidimensional disorder, which results from a complex interaction of biological, genetic, psychological, sociological and environmental factors. For the last few decades it has become a serious health problem in our modern societies. Throughout the world, about 2000 people kill themselves each day. That's about 80 per hour, three quarters of a million a year. Suicide is among the top 10 causes of death in every country, and one of the three leading causes of death in the 15 to 35-year age group. The psychological and social impact of suicide on the family and society is immeasurable. On average, single suicide intimately affects at least six other people. If a suicide occurs in a school or workplace it has an impact on hundreds of people.

To identify, assess and manage suicidal patients is an important task of physicians and psychiatrists, who have a crucial role in suicide prevention. Studies from both developing and developed countries reveal an overall prevalence of mental disorders of 80-100% in cases of completed suicide. It is estimated that the lifetime risk of suicide in people with mood disorders is 6-15%; with alcoholism, 7-15%; and with schizophrenia, 4-10%. However, a substantial proportion of people who commit suicide die without having seen a mental health professional. Hence improved detection, referral and management of psychiatric disorders in primary care is an important step in suicide prevention.

This book provides a comprehensive account of the state of current knowledge concerning incidence of suicide and attempted suicide. It describes the biological, genetic, psychological, and sociological factors related to suicidal behaviour. It also discusses assessment, treatment, and prevention. Specific populations are discussed in detail, including children, adolescents, the elderly, the physically ill, and psychiatric inpatients. It will serve as a highly useful reference too for anyone, including physicians, nurses, social workers, counsellors, teachers, clergy, and parents interested in learning more about suicide.

Editor

1

Understanding Suicide

Over 90 percent of people who die by suicide have a mental illness at the time of their death. And the most common mental illness is depression. Untreated depression is the number one cause for suicide.

Untreated mental illness (including depression, bipolar disorder, shcizophrenia, and others) is the cause for the vast majority of suicides. Also, some people are genetically predisposed to depression, and thus they may not appear to be undergoing any negative life experiences, yet still become depressed, and may die by suicide.

So, some people die by suicide because of a depression that was caused by genetics. You probably have heard about some indivuduals who died by suicide and did not exhibit any symptoms or appear to have any serious problems. In these cases, it is possible that the person had depression that occured because of this genetic factor.

It is very rare that someone dies by suicide because of one cause. Thus, there are usually several causes, and not just one, for suicide. Many people die by suicide because depression is triggered by several negative life experiences, and the person does not receive treatment, or does not receive effective treatment for the depression. (Some people need to go through several treatments until they find one that works for them.)

Some of the negative life experiences that may cause depression, and some other causes for depression, include:

— The death of a loved one.

— A divorce, separation, or breakup of a relationship.

— Losing custody of children, or feeling that a child custody decision is not fair.

— A serious loss, such as a loss of a job, house, or money.

— A serious illness.

— A terminal illness.

— A serious accident.

— Chronic physical pain.

— Intense emotional pain.

— Loss of hope.

— Being victimized (domestic violence, rape, assault, etc).

— A loved one being victimized (child murder, child molestation, kidnapping, murder, rape, assault, etc.).

— Physical abuse.

— Verbal abuse.

— Sexual abuse.

— Unresolved abuse (of any kind) from the past.

— Feeling "trapped" in a situation perceived as negative.

— Feeling that things will never "get better."

— Feeling helpless.

— Serious legal problems, such as criminal prosecution or incarceration.

— Feeling "taken advantage of."

— Inability to deal with a perceived "humiliating" situation.

— Inability to deal with a perceived "failure."

— Alcohol abuse.

— Drug abuse.

— A feeling of not being accepted by family, friends, or society.

— A horrible disappointment.

— Feeling like one has not lived up to his or her high expectations or those of another.

— Bullying. (Adults, as well as children, can be bullied).

— Low self-esteem.

Impact of Racism, Homophobia and Poverty

Gay and lesbian adolescents are overlapping members of two populations that are at high-risk for suicide: youths and homosexuals. Studies among a sample composed predominantly of white gay and lesbian youth demonstrated that a high rate of suicide attempts and suicide ideation -20% and 55%, respectively, - deserved attention from public health officials. Thus, it is clear that sexual orientation is associated with suicidal ideation and suicidal attempts.

The association between sexual orientation and suicidal ideation is strongly supported by other empirical studies identifying the roots of the mental health problems. In a predominantly white sample of gay male youth from the Pacific Northwest and the northern Midwest states, a study found that about one third of the subjects reported at least one suicide attempt. Also, the results indicated that about half of the participants tried more than once to commit suicide. Not surprisingly, about one third of the subjects reported that their suicide attempts had roots in their personal issues about their homosexual identity. Suicide is thus shown to be strongly rooted in personal and interpersonal adaptation to sexual orientation.

Risk Factors

Besides homophobia being a risk factor, lesbian and gay youth are involved in substance and drug abuse, which increases the risk of suicide ideation. Studies have cited alcoholism as a risk factor among gays and lesbians. Drug abuse has also been shown to increase the associated high-risk for suicide among this predominantly adult sample.

Among gay youth, paternal alcoholism has been shown to play a role as a risk factor for suicide ideation. Up to 60% of the gay youth who considered suicide reported an alcoholic father in the sample. Physical violence from alcoholic fathers may ignite suicidal consideration among gay male youth. In terms of coping with daily stressors, gay male youth may have personal difficulties as a result of paternal alcoholism. The decrease of support among friends and family members usually damages a "buffer system" that protects the individual in adverse situations. Lacking a strong relationship also weakens this mechanism.

Non-association roles may also serve as a risk factor among gay and bisexual youth. Male youth that follow a non-conformity trend in relation to gender roles tend to be at a higher risk for suicidal ideation. And those who attempted suicide, they reflected more feminine characteristics in terms of behavior and appearance. Curtis D. Proctor and Victor K. Groze reported similar findings in which feminine gay male youth tended to report more suicide attempts than those who adapted more traditional male gender characteristics. Gay youth that appeared not to conform to stereotypical gender roles are more likely to suffer verbal and physical abuse.

A structural model view indicated that victimization that leads to lower self-esteem might be a strong predictor of suicide ideation in this high-risk population. Self-esteem has been identified as a strong predictor of emotional distress among gay and lesbian youth. Not only does victimization play a role in suicidal consideration, the intensity of the verbal or physiçal abuse does as well. Verbal slurs may play less of a role in terms of intensity, as compared to physical assault. Thus, a homophobic environment that causes lower self-esteem and psychological distress can predict, in turn, a higher risk of suicidality.

Sexual abuse has been indicated to be a risk factor among gay youth. Adolescents who reported suicidal considerations were more likely to have a past of sexual abuse. For example, gay and lesbian youth reported cases of being tricked or forced to have sex. Gay youth that were sexually molested have shown higher rates of HIV risk sexual behavior. Remafedi, Farrow and Persher also reported finding a link between a history of sexual abuse and high-risk of suicide ideation. In the study, suicide attempters were more likely to state a past of sexual abuse in the study. Not only does sexual abuse play a role as a risk factor for HIV intervention, but it also has been associated with higher rates of suicide ideation among gay male youth.

Minority gay males have expressed other life stressors that may place them at a higher risk than their European American counterparts. Minority youth were assumed to experience more risk factors in the Report of the Secretary's Task Force on Youth Suicide, which stated that religion and the family were the most important. Family members may expect gay and lesbian youth to follow their social roles and extend their respective families through heterosexual unions. The report indicated that poverty and racism might be crucial risk factors for gay and lesbian minority adolescents. The report asserted that ethnic minority youth were more likely to attempt suicide because they are a minority in an overwhelmingly white, homophobic society.

Latino gay and bisexual youth expressed their distress of being a "minority within a minority". Thus, racism may play a role in the consideration of suicide. In contrast to the rest of the population, Latino young gay men showed a higher tendency to think about suicide than their European American counterparts. Being a Latino and gay or bisexual has been labeled as a "double jeopardy" because Latinos are less likely to have access to.Hresources that may ensure more psychological support in the United States.

Even though research studies have shown that gay, bisexual and lesbian individuals are at a higher risk for suicide than the general heterosexual population, many of these studies suffer from gaps. First, many of the studies cited do include a large number of subjects. Larger samples are needed to effectively generalize to the rest of the population. Some of the samples were drawn from individuals referred by mental health professionals. These clinical samples who are clinically diagnosed, do not represent the total gay population. Secondly, the research tool used by many of the studies typically measures suicidal ideation in an individual's life, including a distant past.

People have taken their own lives in countries around the world for many centuries. Notions of what suicide means and what to do about it have varied, but at the present time the rates of suicide and suicide attempts in adolescents and young people, are of concern. Recently, however, knowledge and strategies have become available to approach suicide as a preventable public health problem with opportunities to save many lives.

At the present time suicide is the third leading cause of death for persons 15 through 24 years of age, after motor vehicle accidents and homicide. Before the mid-1970s adolescent suicide was a rare event; now nearly a half million teens make a suicide attempt each year. From the 1950s through the 1980s the incidence of suicide among adolescents and young adults nearly tripled. Although the rate in males has decreased over the past decade, the lower suicide rate in female teens has not changed. The actual statistics may be higher because some of these deaths are labeled accidents.

For every completed suicide, an estimated 8 to 25 suicide attempts occur. The results of the 1995 National Youth Risk Behavior Survey of students in grades 7 through 12 indicated that nearly onefourth of students had seriously considered attempting suicide during the 23 months preceding the survey, nearly 18 percent had made a specific plan and nearly 9 percent had made an attempt.

Methods of suicide

The most commonly used methods for suicide are firearms, hanging, poisoning, (overdoses), and jumping. Males tend to use more violent and irreversible methods; females more often will overdose on drugs or slit their wrists. In the latter two methods, there is a greater chance of someone taking corrective action, which may account for the fact that more males than females complete suicide attempts.

The suicide rate among children under the age of 10 is very low, but rises in adolescence. Several studies have shown that elementary school children do indeed have suicidal thoughts and feelings, but several factors protect them from acting on these feelings. Young children

— usually have close relationships with their parents and teachers and receive emotional support,

— have an immature cognitive understanding of the concept of death,

— are limited in their ability to plan the suicidal act and to make decisions regarding the method to be used, and

— have low rates of depression.

Adolescence for many is a stressful time, and ages 13 and 14 are peak periods for suicide attempts. Among older adolescents, between 8 and 10 percent have attempted suicide, with 5 percent sustaining an injury and 2 to 3 percent seeking medical attention. Teenagers tend to communicate less with their parents and have less opportunity to develop supportive relationships with particular teachers. For most teenagers, adolescence is a period marked by role experimentation that will hopefully lead to the development of a sense of personal identity. Adolescence, however, can lead to confusion, isolation, and alienation and can result in drug and alcohol abuse, sexual promiscuity, and a sense of hopelessness and helplessness for some teenagers.

In the U. S., at age 10-to-14-years boys commit suicide almost three times more often than girls; at age 15-to-19 five times more often, and at 20-to-24 almost ten times more often. This means that one female commits suicide for every four males. These gender differences may be due to the fact that suicide is often associated with aggressive behavior, which is more common in males. The strong social connectedness of girls is an additional protective factor.

Suicide rates among whites are higher than among blacks at all ages, including the teen years. Although the risk is greatest among young white males, from 1980 through 1995, suicide rates increased most rapidly among young black males. Native- American males had the highest suicide rate; African American females, the lowest. Ethnic differences may be due to selective under-reporting among minorities.

Certain cultural traditions also play a part; for example, some cultures reduce taboos against suicide (e.g.,

Japanese or Apache Indians). Those cultures that regard suicide in a negative light might inhibit individuals from committing suicide. Religious adherence might decrease suicidal behavior by increasing avenues of social support or through its teachings of personal responsibility.

Sexual orientation

Homosexual and bisexual youth have a high rate of attempted suicide. A statewide survey of students in grades 7 through 12 indicated that 28.1 percent of bisexual and homosexual males and 20.5 percent of bisexual and homosexual females had reported attempting suicide. Although gay, lesbian and bisexual youth have higher rates of suicidal ideation and suicide attempts, their risk for completed suicide has not yet been determined.

Family functioning

Research indicates that suicide victims communicate less often and less fully with their parents than other teens, and they are somewhat more likely to come from a broken home than other youngsters of the same ethnic group, although the overall impact of separation/divorce is small. Marital or parent/child friction, in and of themselves, do not appear to affect suicide risk. A high proportion of teens who commit or attempt suicide have had a close family member (parent, sibling, aunt, uncle or grandparent) or friend who attempted or committed suicide. The relative contributions of identification with the deceased (modeling suicidal behavior as an acceptable response to solving problems) versus heredity have yet to be clarified.

Psychiatric diagnoses are almost always part of the suicide victim's profile; psychological autopsy studies show

90% of these teenagers had a psychiatric disorder. The most common diagnoses are:

Mood disorder	60%
Antisocial disorder	50%
Substance abuse	35%
Anxiety disorder	27%

Only a small number of suicides occur in teenagers with schizophrenia or manicdepression. Depression alone or in combination with aggressive behavior and/or substance abuse or anxiety has been found in over half of all suicide victims. Alcohol and drug abuse have been present in approximately two-thirds of 18- to 19-year-old males, but are not common in younger males or female suicide victims. Previous suicide attempts were made by approximately one-third of teenage suicide victims.

Thoughts of hopelessness, often characteristic of depression, are common in adolescents contemplating suicide. These adolescents believe that things will never get better; they find it difficult to understand that depressed feelings are temporary and will abate. They perceive themselves to be the cause of negative events, believe they have no control over what happens to them, and that nothing they do will change things. This bleak view of the future, combined with an impulsive style, may influence suicidal behavior.

Suicidal behavior is known to run in families and can exist whether or not other inherited conditions such as depression and schizophrenia are diagnosed in a family member. Genes could be responsible for neurobiological differences that appear to influence the expression of behavior. In particular, low serotonin, a neurotransmitter, has been shown to play a role in those who are suicidal. Cerebrospinal fluid, postmortem brain autopsies, and neuroimaging studies, have shown that low serotonin is associated with a lower threshold to acting on both suicidal and aggressive impulses. Females, who generally have higher levels of serotonin metabolites, have lower rates of both aggressive behavior and high lethality suicide attempts.

Low cholesterol diets result in lower serotonergic activity and increased aggression in nonhuman primates. Although there appears to be an increase in suicide risk with low serum cholesterol in humans, a direct effect of cholesterol on serotonergic activity has yet to be demonstrated. Change in the response of stress related hormones (cortisol) to testing via the Dexamethasone Suppression Test has been implicated as a marker for subtypes of depression and possibly likelihood of suicide in adults. A goal of future neurobiological research is to develop biologic screening tests for adults and children with predictive value that will allow for the design and implementation of specific prevention efforts.

Suicide is the result of the interaction among seemingly disparate factors. It often occurs when an individual with a longterm predisposition experiences a stressful event. The act of suicide requires both a stressor (precipitant or trigger) as well as an underlying vulnerability (diathesis) towards acting on suicidal thoughts. A recent distressing event may set off a longstanding vulnerability. The interaction of a psychiatric disorder, substance abuse, a recent stress, inadequate support, and feelings of hopelessness may lead to suicide for some teenagers.

Studies show that the following stresses occurred in the lives of teenagers who committed suicide:

— Disciplinary crisis - suspension from school, appearance in juvenile court

— Relationship problem - breakup with girl or boyfriend; rejection by a friend

— School failure

— Humiliation

— Pregnancy

Clearly, not all teenagers who endure such experiences resort to suicide. Only a few of all youngsters who have a psychiatric disorder, a stressful event, inadequate support and a hopeless view of life actually commit suicide. What makes the difference? What factors might facilitate the likelihood of suicide?

— Personality traits such as impulsivity

— Biological traits such as neurochemical imbalances

— Lack of strong family ties

— Social factors such as absence of strong taboos, social isolation and recent occurrence of suicide

— Method availability (easy access to firearms) and familiarity

— Agitated mental state

What factors might inhibit or protect a person from committing suicide?

— Strong family and social support

— Religious taboos

— Good grades

— Presence of others

— Difficulty of access to method

— Slowed down, rather than agitated, mental state

Intervention and treatment

The adolescent who has made a suicide attempt or is showing the warning signs leading to suicidal behavior needs to have his or her illness recognized and diagnosed and appropriate treatment plans formulated. A treatment plan should be based on an evaluation that includes assessment of the adolescent's mental state and the nature of family interactions. When a teenager who has made a suicide attempt is brought to a hospital emergency room hospital admission may be warranted to insure safety.

Psychopharmacologic treatment Psychopharmacologic treatment of suicidal behavior involves treatment of associated psychiatric disorders. Antidepressants (tricyclic TCAs); monoamine oxidase inhibitors (MAOIs); and selective serotonin reuptake inhibitors (SSRIs) are useful in the treatment of depression in adults. One cannot directly extrapolate from adult data since depressed adolescents have not derived the same benefits from TCAs. There is supportive evidence for the benefits of SSRIs in adolescent depression. Given their efficacy, lack of lethality during intentional overdose, ease of use (no need for therapeutic blood level monitoring and electrocardiograms) and relative lack of side effects compared to TCAs, SSRIs are first line agents in the treatment of adolescent depression.

Mood stabilizers (lithium, valproate) are used with patients with bipolar disorders but have also not been assessed in randomized controlled trials with adolescents. Fluvoxamine, an SSRI, has been shown to be effective in the treatment of children and adolescents with social phobia, separation anxiety disorder and generalized anxiety disorder. There are no current medication strategies that directly treat suicidal behavior, although there is suggestive evidence with adults that medicines which increase serotonin may be protective against suicide attempts. There is intriguing epidemiologic evidence of decreasing suicide rates in Sweden and in white adolescent males in the U.S. over the past decade paralleling the exponential increase in prescriptions for antidepressants, particularly SSRIs, over the same time frame. Although SSRIs have been shown to decrease suicidal ideation in both depressed and nondepressed adults with borderline personality disorder, their impact on reducing future suicide attempts is less robust.

Psychological treatment

There are few controlled studies of adolescents who attempt suicide which would lead to the design of optimal treatment approaches. It is customary to use a problem-oriented approach that addresses the diagnosis, the circumstances that led to the attempt and the family situation. Cognitive-behavior therapy (CBT) aims to help the teen identify negative feeling states, correct irrational ideas and become aware of the available options. For example, if suicide is seen as the "only solution" to a "hopeless" problem, the therapist will help the teen balance reasons for living and dying, teach alternative problemsolving solutions, and through the use of role-playing, rehearse strategies that can be used in a crisis situation.

Dialectical behavior therapy (DBT), currently used with at-risk adults with borderline personality disorder, is being modified for use with adolescents. This approach, based on a combined motivational and skill deficit model, has been found useful with individuals who are vulnerable to intense reactions but have deficits in regulation of emotions. Interpersonal therapy (IPT) is based on the premise that the symptoms of depression occur in an interpersonal context.

Treatment focuses on training the teen to learn strategies to develop, assess and respond to relationships in context. Family counseling is recommended to reduce parent-child conflict and to improve family communication and conflictresolution skills. Improved family relations often reduce the teen's feelings of hopelessness and anger. Group therapy may be used when there is a need to reduce a sense of isolation or to provide peer support and opportunities to share problems. However, given the evidence that suicide may sometimes be a modeled behavior, groups with attempters should be organized and run with caution by skilled and experienced professionals.

What Can You do to Prevent Suicide

There are many things that can be done. Free Suicide Prevention Program is being used by schools throughout the world. It is easy to implement, and it does not cost anything. All schools need to have a suicide prevention program. Also, the suicide prevention program can be used by any organization or group that would benefit from it.

So there are five things that you can do right now to help prevent suicide.

— You are the people who will take action in your communities to prevent suicide.

— You will spearhead the suicide prevention programs.

— You will put up the signs on bulletin boards.

— You will learn more about suicide.

— You will help remove the stigma from suicide.

The National Strategy for Suicide Prevention, a public-private undertaking launched on May 2, 2001 by the U. S. Surgeon General David Satcher, lays the foundation of a national strategy to confront this serious public health problem. The goals are to:

— promote awareness that suicide is a public health problem that is preventable

— develop and implement strategies to reduce the stigma associated with being a consumer of mental health, substance abuse and suicide prevention services

— develop and implement communitybased suicide prevention programs that build life skills and connections to family and community support

— promote efforts to reduce access to lethal means and methods of self-harm

— implement training for recognition of at-risk behavior and delivery of effective treatment. Medical and other professionals should be trained in screening adolescents at-risk

— identify and refer at-risk teenagers. A screening program to identify those who have made previous attempts or who are currently suicidal should be implemented

— develop and promote effective clinical and professional practices by establishing a uniform system for hospitals, policy-makers and professionals to identify and report suicides

— increase access to and community linkages with mental health and substance abuse services. The number of states that require health insurance plans to cover mental health issues on the same level as physical illness should be increased

— improve media reporting and portrayals of suicidal behavior, mental illness and substance abuse. For example, broadcasters should run public service ads such as those on children's car seats, smoking or drinking while pregnant. It is important that the media not minimize the role of mental illness, romanticize or glamorize the suicides of celebrities or describe methods in precise detail. These techniques are likely to lessen contagion effects

— promote and support research on suicide and suicide prevention

Role of Parents

A teen's statement of a wish to kill him/ herself must be taken seriously. Before actually committing or attempting suicide, teens often make direct statements about their intention to end their lives, or less direct statements about how they might as well be dead or that their friends and families would be better off without them. Don't worry that discussing the problem will encourage the teenager to go through with the plan. On the contrary, it will help him or her to know that someone is willing to be a friend. It may save a life. Watch for symptoms of depression, which may include:

— a change in eating and sleeping habits

— a marked personality change, exhibiting angry actions or rebellious behavior or withdrawal from friends and regular activities involvement in drugs or alcohol or other risky behaviors such as reckless driving

— an over-reaction to a recent humiliating experience

— difficulty in concentration and a decline in the quality of school work

— persistent boredom and/or lethargy

— unusual neglect of appearance complaints about physical symptoms such as headaches, stomachaches and fatigue

— a pattern of giving away or throwing away possessions

— intolerance of praise or rewards

— preoccupation with death in writing songs or poems

— an increase in comments such as "I can't take it anymore" or "Nobody cares; I wish I was dead."

Depression and suicidal feelings are treatable mental disorders. With support from family and community resources and professional treatment, teenagers and young adults who show suicidal behavior can be helped, tragic actions prevented, and healthier behaviors established.

Almost all suicidal behavior occurs in the context of a mental disorder. The risk is elevated further when mental disorders are complicated by substance use. These well-documented findings carry significant implications for prevention strategies. Perhaps most importantly, our knowledge that mental disorders and substance abuse contribute to suicide risk has helped raise awareness that adequate detection and treatment of mental disorders can truly be a life or death issue.

Despite the 30,000 lives that suicide claims each year, and despite the searing intensity of the act of suicide - for family members and other survivors, as well as for the victim of an attempted or completed suicide - the relative infrequency of suicide in the population at large was long believed to have stymied attempts to identify specific, reliable risk factors.

Follow-up studies of adults with mental or substance abuse disorders reveal the inordinately high risk of suicide associated with these disorders. Some 30 years ago, Guze and Robins documented that patients who had been hospitalized for affective disorders had an alarmingly high rate of suicide and subsequently estimated that persons with depression had a lifetime risk for suicide of 15 percent. Since their work, numerous other studies have followed other patients with depression - including less severely ill patients who had been treated in outpatient as well as inpatient settings - for longer periods of time.

Although the revised estimates from this research are less dismal, the lifetime risk for suicide is still 6 times higher for persons with a diagnosable depression than for a person without the illness. Among persons with schizophrenia, over the typically life-long course of this illness, the risk for suicide is between 4- and 6 percent, but with risk higher earlier in the course of illness. Approximately 7 percent of those with alcohol dependence will die by suicide. Persons with mental disorders who attempt suicide are at significantly elevated risk - 3 to 7 times greater than others with the same illnesses - for eventually completing suicide. In the U.S. population at large, an "average" American, has less than a 1 percent likelihood of dying by suicide.

Clinical risk "profiles" vary by age and gender. For example, among adolescent male suicide victims, the most common profile is depression, complicated by a pattern of problematic behavior at home and in school, including alcohol or other substance abuse, that often leads to isolation and rejection. Among adolescent females, a mood disorder is most likely, with conduct problems and substance abuse less likely. Among older white males--that is, men 55 and older, who comprise the group with the highest rates of suicide, at six times the national average--alcohol use is very infrequent, and a moderately severe, late onset depression is most common. More so than among other age groups, depression in the elderly is often obscured by symptoms of physical illness, and by loss and loneliness that all too often mar late life; thus depression is not recognized or treated adequately.

Different Risk Factor

Because different age and gender groups seem to have different risk factor profiles. Following are some current treatment and prevention efforts for reduction of suicidal behavior within specific age groups.

Global Perspective of Suicide Rates

Global suicide rates and trends are presented, highlighting particularities of different countries indifferent regions of the world. The global data are examined with regards to sex, age and in relation to cultural factors (i.e. the prevailing religion) in countries. With regards to the prevention of suicide, the necessity of a local system of monitoring suicide trends is stressed.

Since its foundation in 1948, the World Health Organization (WHO) has been collaborating with its Member States in view of perfecting methods for obtaining, processing and analysing data on mortality and morbidity. As a result, WHO maintains a data bank on mortality according to the data provided by its Member States. Deaths from all causes are reported, usually split by sex and age, along with mid-year population data. The actual number of deaths in each demographic category is then transformed into rates. The WHO data bank on mortality has grown from a few Member States in the early 1950s to more than 100 Member States that reported at some point in time.

Mortality associated with suicide is part of the data bank. The regularity of reporting on mortality has been varied. Some Member States have been reporting data since 1950 (11 countries); others do not report at all. In 1985, the largest number of countries reported on mortality (74 countries) and by 1998 there were still 50 countries involved. Almost no data is available from the WHO African Region, scarce information from the WHO South-East Asia and Eastern Mediterranean Regions, and irregular information is sent from many countries of the Western Pacific Region and from Latin American countries of the Region of the Americas. From countries of the European Region data are received mostly on a regular basis.

It is of special relevance to the field of suicidology that the category name and code of mortality associated with suicide has remained relatively stable through successive editions of the International Statistical Classification of Diseases and Related Health Problems (ICD), from 1CD-G to ICD-10.

According to WHO estimates for the year 2020 and based on current trends, approximately 1.53 million people will die from suicide, and 10-20 times more people will attempt suicide worldwide. This represents on average one death every 20 seconds and one attempt every 1-2 seconds. Although it is customary in the suicidology literature to present rates of suicide for both men and women combined (the so called total suicide rates), it should be noted that the current general epidemiological practice is to present rates according to sex and age, particularly when important differences (in terms of figures or risk factors) across sex or age groups exist. This is precisely the situation in relation to suicide; suicide rates of men and women are consistently different in most places, as are rates in different age groups.

The highest suicide rates for both men and women are found in Europe, more particularly in Eastern Europe, in a group of countries that share similar historical and sociocultural characteristics, such as Estonia, Latvia, Lithuania and, to a lesser extent, Finland, Hungary and the Russian Federation. Nevertheless some similarly high rates are found in countries that are quite distinct in relation to these characteristics, such as Sri Lanka and Cuba.

Curiously enough, when the data are separated by WHO region, the highest rates in each region with the exception of Europe, are found in island countries, such as Cuba, Japan, Mauritius and Sri Lanka. Also, according to the WHO regional distribution, the lowest rates as a whole are found in the Eastern Mediterranean Region, which comprises mostly countries that follow Islamic traditions; this is also true of some Central Asian republics that had formerly been integrated into the Soviet Union.

Global suicide rates (per 100,000 population) have been calculated starting from 1950. Deaths reported by countries in each year were averaged and projected in relation to the global population over 5 years of age at each respective year. An increase of approximately 49% for suicide rates in males and 33% for suicide rates in females can be observed between 1950 and 1995.

The increase in these global suicide rates must be interpreted with caution. On the one hand it might reflect fact that since the end of USSR which had an overall rate below the average), some of its former republics (particularly those with the highest rates in the world) started to report individually, thus inflating the global rate. On the other hand, figures for 1950 were based on 11 countries only, and this gradually increased up to 1995, when the estimates were based on 62 countries that reported on suicide. These 62 countries as a whole probably have higher rates, they are more concerned with them and they have a higher tendency to report on suicide mortality than countries where suicide is not perceived as a major public health problem. There is only one exception (China), where suicide rates in females are consistently higher than suicide rates in males, particularly in rural areas.

As for age, there is a clear tendency for suicide rates to increase with age. Against a global suicide rate of 26.9 deaths per 100,000 for men in 1998, the rates for specific age groups start at 1.2 (in the age group 5-14 years) and gradually increase up to 55.7 (in the age group over 75 years). The same positive relationship between age and suicide rates is observed in relation to suicide rates in females: for an overall rate of 8.2 in 1998, specific age group rates grow from 0.5 per 100,000 (in the age group 5-14 years) to 18.8 (in the age group over 75 years).

Absolute numbers of suicide

In spite of the wide (and appropriate) use of rates, the information conveyed by them alone can be misleading, particularly when comparing data across countries or regions with important differences in the demographic structure. As indicated earlier, the highest suicide rates are currently reported in Eastern Europe; however, the largest numbers of suicides are found in Asia.

Given the size of their population, almost 30% of all cases of suicide worldwide are committed in China and India alone, although the suicide rate of China practically coincides with the global average and that of India is almost half of the global suicide rate. The number of suicides in China alone is 30% greater than the total number of suicides in the whole of Europe, and the number of suicides in India alone (the second highest) is equivalent to those in the four European countries with the highest number of suicides together (Russia, Germany, France and Ukraine).

Given the relatively narrow differences in the population of males and females in each age group, the large predominance of suicide rates among males is also found in relation to the actual number of suicides committed. It is in relation to age, however, that the most striking changes in the picture are perceived when we move from rates to total numbers. Although suicide rates can be between six and eight times higher among the elderly, as compared with young people, currently more young people than elderly people are dying from suicide, globally speaking. Currently, more suicides (55%) are committed by people aged 5-44 years than by people aged 45 years and older. Also, the age group in which most suicides are currently completed is 35-44 years for both men and women.

This 'ungreying' of suicide is a relatively new phenomenon. It becomes dramatic when one considers that the proportion of the elderly in the total population is increasing at a greater rate than the one of younger people. Also, it is not the result of a divergent modification in suicide rates in these age groups: the suicide rate in young people is increasing at a greater pace than it is in the elderly.

A comparison of suicide rates according to the prevalent religious denomination in countries brings to light a most remarkable difference between countries of Islam and countries of any other prevailing religion. In Muslim countries (e.g. Kuwait), where committing suicide is most strictly forbidden, the total suicide rate is close to zero (0.1 per 100,000 population). In Hindu (e.g. India) and Christian countries (e.g. Italy), the total suicide rate is around 10 per 100,000 (Hindu: 9.6; Christian: 11.2).

2

Sociology of Suicide

A sociocultural perspective provides an important counterpoint to the dominant medical and psychological approaches to suicide, which do not fully explore the relation between the self and the social. Much research into the nature of youth suicide has been undertaken by psychiatrists and adolescent mental health researchers who have been concerned with the problem of mental health/ illness and identifying individual pathology.

Yet, we don't really know how suicide is conceptualised by young people themselves - it may not be that a discourse of mental health figures in their understandings and if this is so, we need to consider the language and conceptual basis of suicide prevention programs and policies. Furthermore, discourses about suicide as primarily a mental health problem may well serve to frame a young person's emotional distress in terms of psychological problems, and so discount the sociocultural factors and the ways in which that distress is managed.

More recently, the significance of social factors which affect the lives and deaths of young people have been recognised through epidemiological research. For example, unemployment, geographic location, gender, homelessness, family difficulties, mental illness and previous suicide attempts. Sociologists have also contributed to the understanding of suicide as a social phenomenon. However, this research tends to use quantified measures, statistics and generalised causation theories. While this quantitative approach is useful in the evaluation of broad cultural trends and for examining the correlation between social factors and suicide, it does not allow for the exploration of the complex everyday meanings and social relationships governing the suicidal behaviour of individuals within their communities.

Hassan argues that to understand the motivated nature of suicide, one not only needs to explore the external social factors but also how these factors are internal to the suicidal individual. Often the term "social factors" confuses (1) the social causes, and (2) sociocultural conceptualisations, the former referring to the individual's social context, the latter emphasising the way in which such "factors" are discursively understood.

Social factors such as unemployment or sexual orientation do not cause suicide in some determinate way. Rather, they are factors mediated by the sociocultural conceptualisations (or discourses) through which the individual experiences them. These meanings transmitted in the form of everyday stories, media reports and narratives about oneself, shape the way young people construct their identity and whether or not they act in a self-violent manner in times of emotional distress.

Within the transitional time of acquiring an adult identity, the question of sexuality arises as a significant experience that generates many conflicting issues for young people within their communities. Sexuality involves the dimensions of self which include: gendered identity, self-image, sexual orientation, negotiating intense relationships and rejection/acceptance by oneself, family and community members.

Research suggests that young gay/lesbian/bisexual people experience homophobia and marginalisation, both of which are associated with increased risk of suicide attempts. In an American study, Remfedi found that one third of suicide attempts in his study occurred in the same year that the young person identified as gay or lesbian. The issue of sexuality and identity is not limited to gay or lesbian young people, but rather is a dimension of self that all young people negotiate through the customs, discourses and taboos of their culture.

The issues raised above identify the significant connection between youth suicide and the process of identity formation, enacted in the roles and stories that constitute everyday life - in the domains of home, leisure and recreation, work or unemployment, study and the many other aspects of youth culture. From this perspective, suicide raises important conceptual and practical issues of how young people experience and negotiate marginalisation - the power relations which govern the spatial organisation of everyday life and significant relationships.

For example, a young person's experience of alienating environments is significant in how they develop social networks and relate to themselves and within their community. Leisure, cultural and social opportunities are vital in developing a young person's sense of belonging in relation to place, whether in an urban or regional context.

Paradoxical Nature of Suicide

The implementation of suicide is often one of the most private of all human actions, yet its impact on the people left behind could not be more profound. Self-destruction frequently crosses the minds of vast numbers of humans, but it remains among the most taboo of topics. Mental health professionals encourage the public to feel comfortable discussing suicidal thoughts, yet many of these same professionals are hesitant to ask family members or colleagues whether they are having such thoughts.

Death is sometimes chosen as the only alternative by people who feel deeply alone or shamed, yet are profoundly loved and respected. The manner of suicide adds to the paradox. If a businessman takes his life in an effort to avoid scandal and the pain of admitting his wrongdoing to his family, he may be labeled as a coward; yet a soldier who jumps on a land mine to save fellow troops will undoubtedly be called a hero.

The paradoxical nature of suicide has not been lost on philosophers. Arthur Schopenhauer cogently captured the essence of the most ironic paradox of the suicidal act:

Suicide may also be regarded as an experiment-a question which man puts to Nature, trying to force her to answer. The question is this: What change will death produce in a man's existence and ir. his insight into the nature of things? It is a clumsy experiment to make, for it involves the destruction of the very consciousness which puts the question and awaits the answer.

Its paradoxical nature is one of the reasons that exploration and discussion of suicide, within the clinical interview, raise such powerful emotions in both patients and clinicians. Some of its greatest paradoxes still await us. They will surface as we begin to more carefully explore the nature of suicide by looking, first, at its epidemiology and then at some of the practical problems inherent in its prediction.

Suicide is one of our most pressing public health concerns. In the United States, suicide is the ninth leading cause of death in adults, with 30,903 suicides in 1996. It has been estimated that a suicide occurs every twenty minutes. In the age group of 15 to 25 years, suicide is the third leading cause of death in America. Between 1952 and 1992, the rate of suicide among adolescents and young adults tripled. And even though young children are much less likely to commit suicide, they still do. In the United States in 1995, 330 children, ages 10 to 14, killed themselves and seven children, ages 5 to 9, committed suicide.

The development of improved ways of spotting and providing relief to acutely suicidal patients could dramatically decrease one of the leading causes of death in both the United States and the world at large. As a society, we must openly address suicide as a public health problem and, as was done with smoking, aggressively address methods of decreasing its prevalence.

Several studies have shown that roughly 50 percent of people who commit suicide have been seen by a primary care physician within the month prior to their death. This staggering statistic provides hope. If effective screening mechanisms can be developed and are subsequently embraced and effectively utilized by primary care physicians, a marked drop in suicide could result. This is not a pipe dream. It can happen.

But the task is formidable. Some studies shows that clinicians have little ability to predict imminent suicide. For a moment, let us look at this problem of prediction more carefully. What are some of the factors that might help us to predict that a person is not acutely suicidal? In essence, what are the risk factors and what does the absence of these risk factors mean?

Suicide Assessment

The art of suicide assessment is composed of three tasks:

(1) gathering information related to the risk factors for suicide,

(2) gathering information related to the patient's suicidal ideation and planning, and

(3) the clinical decision making that is subsequently applied to these two databases.

Errors can occur in any of these three tasks. Much attention has been given to the first and third tasks. Curiously, much less attention has been given to the practical art of eliciting suicidal ideation and planning itself. For years, the vogue has been the development of instruments for statistical analysis of risk factors.

But people don't kill themselves because statistics suggest that they should. The call to suicide comes not from statistical protocol, but from psychological pain. Each person is unique. Statistical power is at its best when applied to large populations, and at its weakest when applied to individuals. But it is the individual who clinicians must assess in the quietude of their offices or the distracting hubbub of busy emergency rooms.

It is from the patient's individual world, the intimate world of his or her own phenomenology, that suicide is conceived as the correct answer. An obvious point warrants repeating: Most people kill themselves because they decide to kill themselves. A given individual can present with very few risk factors, but if that patient has decided to kill himself or herself, that patient will-and the absence of risk factors be damned. Another patient may have an enormous number of risk factors, but if that patient does not want to kill himself or herself, no suicide will occur. No formal risk factor analysis will help us here, any more than it did in the reading of Sylvia Plath's letter to her mother.

Granted, some clients inadvertently kill themselves when a suicidal gesture backfires into a lethal attempt. Other clients, with processes such as borderline pathology, may move with surprising impulsivity into suicide. But these exceptions do not define the rule. Generally, a decision to kill oneself is made after a complex and stressful weighing of the pros and cons by reflective people who would not choose death as the answer if life provided better solutions. The actual behaviors that end life-swallowing pills, pulling triggers, stringing ropes are preceded by an intricate array of thoughts devoted to the implementation of these plans. These thoughts shape, and ultimately determine, whether t hese actions will be undertaken.

The sequential unfolding of thought and action, inherent in the process of attempting suicide, offers clinicians a glimmer of hope concerning our attempts at suicide prediction, because it suggests that there are warnings of imminent suicidal action. But these warnings lie deep inside the mind and soul of the client. On one level, an uncovering of the client's internal dialogue, concerning the pros and cons of committing suicide, can provide important clues toward prediction. But on a more practical level, knowledge of the degree of concrete planning and the actions taken on that planning probably serves as a better barometer of how close at hand the act may be. If the clinician is allowed to enter this secretive world of concrete suicidal planning, such an invitation may represent the best window we have into the severity of the client's pain and the proximity of death as an answer to that pain.

Current Perspective of Attempted Suicide

A sociocultural perspective provides an important counterpoint to the dominant medical and psychological approaches to suicide, which do not fully explore the relation between the self and the social. Much research into the nature of youth suicide has been undertaken by psychiatrists and adolescent mental health researchers who have been concerned with the problem of mental health/ illness and identifying individual pathology.

Yet, we don't really know how suicide is conceptualised by young people themselves - it may not be that a discourse of mental health figures in their understandings and if this is so, we need to consider the language and conceptual basis of suicide prevention programs and policies. Furthermore, discourses about suicide as primarily a mental health problem may well serve to frame a young person's emotional distress in terms of psychological problems, and so discount the sociocultural factors and the ways in which that distress is managed.

More recently, the significance of social factors which affect the lives and deaths of young people have been recognised through epidemiological research. For example, unemployment, geographic location, gender, homelessness, family difficulties, mental illness and previous suicide attempts. Sociologists have also contributed to the understanding of suicide as a social phenomenon. However, this research tends to use quantified measures, statistics and generalised causation theories. While this quantitative approach is useful in the evaluation of broad cultural trends and for examining the correlation between social factors and suicide, it does not allow for the exploration of the complex everyday meanings and social relationships governing the suicidal behaviour of individuals within their communities.

Hassan argues that to understand the motivated nature of suicide, one not only needs to explore the external social factors but also how these factors are internal to the suicidal individual. Often the term "social factors" confuses (1) the social causes, and (2) sociocultural conceptualisations, the former referring to the individual's social context, the latter emphasising the way in which such "factors" are discursively understood.

Social factors such as unemployment or sexual orientation do not cause suicide in some determinate way. Rather, they are factors mediated by the sociocultural conceptualisations (or discourses) through which the individual experiences them. These meanings transmitted in the form of everyday stories, media reports and narratives about oneself, shape the way young people construct their identity and whether or not they act in a self-violent manner in times of emotional distress.

Within the transitional time of acquiring an adult identity, the question of sexuality arises as a significant experience that generates many conflicting issues for young people within their communities. Sexuality involves the dimensions of self which include: gendered identity, self-image, sexual orientation, negotiating intense relationships and rejection/acceptance by oneself, family and community members.

Research suggests that young gay/lesbian/bisexual people experience homophobia and marginalisation, both of which are associated with increased risk of suicide attempts. In an American study, Remfedi found that one third of suicide attempts in his study occurred in the same year that the young person identified as gay or lesbian. The issue of sexuality and identity is not limited to gay or lesbian young people, but rather is a dimension of self that all young people negotiate through the customs, discourses and taboos of their culture.

The issues raised above identify the significant connection between youth suicide and the process of identity formation, enacted in the roles and stories that constitute everyday life - in the domains of home, leisure and recreation, work or unemployment, study and the many other aspects of youth culture. From this perspective, suicide raises important conceptual and practical issues of how young people experience and negotiate marginalisation - the power relations which govern the spatial organisation of everyday life and significant relationships.

For example, a young person's experience of alienating environments is significant in how they develop social networks and relate to themselves and within their community. Leisure, cultural and social opportunities are vital in developing a young person's sense of belonging in relation to place, whether in an urban or regional context.

3

Socioeconomic Factors of Suicide

In recent years there has been growing concern over suicide in young people, particularly as the rates have increased in several countries. Young people who commit suicide often have a history of mental illness, a family history of mental illness or suicidal behaviour, or dysfunctional family backgrounds such as divorce or socioeconomic adversity.

Yet the link between family related risk factors and their relative importance in sui. cide in young people is poorly understood because studies have either not included all the factors, using the same methods, or not been population based. Several countries have developed preventive strategies for suicide, and in some of these countries young people are considered an important target group.

Preventive strategies cannot, however, be based on empirical evidence as this does not exist.Current knowledge of risk factors for suicide in young people stems from either studies of risk factors in people that have attempted suicide or studies of psychological autopsy (information collected on the deceased through interviews with family members, relatives, friends, and healthcare staff), in which recall bias cannot be excluded. We aimed to determine the effect of familial, psychiatric, and socioeconomic factors in young people who had committed suicide.

The Danish psychiatric central register includes the dates for admission and discharge and diagnoses for all psychiatric inpatients in Denmark since 1969 according to ICD.8 and ICD.10 codes. No private psychiatric hospitals exist in Denmark, and all treatment is free. The integrated database for longitudinal labour market research contains detailed yearly information for the Danish population from 1980 onwards, with information from administrative registers. Information was only recorded for people living in the country on 31 December, thus excluding those who had emigrated or died within the year.

Overall, 496 young people in Denmark committed suicide during 1981-97. Males were three and a half times more likely to commit suicide than were females, and the number of suicides increased homogeneously with age in both sexes. The risk of suicide was increased among young people with a parental history of suicide, admission for a mental illness, being single, being unemployed (dose. response association), or being a recipient of social benefits, or whose sibling had been admitted with a mental illness, whose mother had died from other causes or had emigrated, or whose father had a poor education or was in the lowest quarter for income.

Risk factors related to the father's socioeconomic background were stronger than those of the mother's, whereas risk factors related to the mother's vital status and admissions for a mental illness were stronger than those of the father's. In the young people themselves a strong association was found between suicide and admission to hospital for mental illnesses, and an inverse association was found between risk of suicide and education.

The effect of the risk factors decreased after adjustment for a family history of admission for a mental illness. This decrease was more pronounced for parental socioeconomic factors and less distinct for factors related to parental vital status and psychiatric history, whereas the effect of individual admission for a mental illness remained the main risk factor. When all factors were considered those for parental suicide or admission for a mental illness or the loss of a mother due to other causes of death or emigration remained significant.

No specific psychiatric diagnosis in a parent was associated with a significantly increased risk of suicide in the offspring. The effects of the parents' job status and education were reduced and non.significant. However, the direction of these factors was similar to that of the crude analysis. These changes were primarily due to confounding between these socioeconomic variables and a family history of admission for mental illness, because the incidence rate ratios were similar to those adjusted for admission for mental illness in the family. A history of admission with a mental illness among the young people was relatively unchanged and remained the strongest risk factor.

The risk of suicide among those admitted with schizophre. nia was significantly higher than that associated with other psychiatric diagnoses, even though young males with other psychiatric diagnoses had a lower risk than young females. Only young females were admitted with affective disorders and eating disorders. The difference between the sexes was also significant among those whose father had been admitted for a mental illness, with only young females having a significantly increased risk. Moreover, individual education remained a protective factor. An interaction with age was only significant in those whose father had been admitted for a mental illness, when the relative risk declined with the subject's age.

The distribution of risk factors and the adjusted relative risk associated with the most significant factors were transformed into attributable risks. If all individuals had a similar risk to those not exposed to individual mental illness, mental illness in a parent, or suicide of a parent, the proportion of suicides that would be prevented was about 30%, of which 15% was attributed to mental illness in the young person.

Domestic Violence

One in three women is victimized by domestic violence at some point in her life. Only one in five victims with physical injuries seeks medical treatment. Only about half of domestic violence incidents are reported to police. Almost all of the perpetrators of domestic violence say that they will stop. But most don't. The violence usually gets worse.

All women who are victims of domestic violence are at risk of being murdered by their abusers. And one out of every four women who are the victims of domestic violence attempt suicide. Domestic violence is always wrong, and it is a crime.

All perpetrators of domestic violence are cowards and criminals. The women who are victimized by these heinous crimes feel trapped and confused. The abuser not only physically attacks the woman, but also psychologically attacks her. The verbal attacks are meant to control the victim, and to try to strip her of her self-esteem, self-confidence, and self-love. The perpetrator also often wants the woman to believe that she is at fault for the violence and the verbal abuse.

Many domestic violence victims try to change their behavior (even though they are not doing anything wrong) because the horrible attacks leave them hopeless, helpless, and confused. But there really is nothing that the victims can do to stop the violence, because they are dealing with a selfish, cruel criminal who does not have a conscience. All of the blame is on the criminal—the cowardly perpetrator of the domestic violence—not on the victim.

The horrible crime of domestic violence often results in a woman isolating herself and becoming clinically depressed. Many women feel trapped and powerless, and do not receive treatment for their depression, and thus believe that suicide is the only way out. Also, many children who are in households where domestic violence occurs attempt suicide. Children are deeply affected by the physical and emotional abuse; they too feel powerless, and oftentimes become depressed. They may seek to end their own pain and escape from the horrors of domestic violence with dying by suicide.

Depression

Sadness is a normal part of our lives. Often, we feel sad because of stressful things that happen to us (the death of a loved one, the breakup of a relationship, serious illness, the loss of a job). Depression is sadness that is much more intense than, or lasts much longer than, the ordinary sadness we might expect to feel under the specific circumstances. Also, while we may feel depressed as a reaction to a specific, stressful event in our lives, we can also be depressed even though no "major" stressful event has happened.

One key difference between depression and ordinary sadness is that depression often impairs our ability to function. Depression results from chemical action in the brain, which is why anti-depressant medications can help treat it.

Someone who suffers from depression is said to be "clinically depressed," or to have a "unipolar disorder." Note that a depressed person may not be depressed all the time, but may simply be depressed at certain times. Some people even have depression that alternates with extreme "up" moods: they are said to have a "bipolar disorder," or be "manic-depressive." Even people with a bi-polar disorder may be depressed enough to be suicidal when they are having a depressive episode.

Depression may have a number of causes including:

—the effects of some medications

—alcohol or drug abuse

—certain diseases

Because of this, it is usually a good idea for someone who suffers from depression to see a doctor to make sure that the depression does not have a medical cause.

Important Things to Know about Depression

—Being depressed does not mean that you are "weak" or "crazy"

—Professional help is very important in dealing with depression

—Depression can be successfully treated with medication and counseling in the large majority of cases

—You can still keep your job even though you are being treated for depression

Anti-Depressant Medications

Anti-depressant medications are usually very effective in treating depression. You should know that:

Your doctor may have to try several different medications to find one that is best for you

A doctor may have a specific anti-depressant medication that he or she usually prescribes first. If this first medication doesn't help, the doctor should try other medications. If there is any question about anti-depressant medications, you should consult a psychiatrist or other doctor who is experienced with anti-depressant medications.

Some medications may take days or weeks to become effective

Because it may take some time for an anti-depressant medication to work, you should not be discouraged if you don't see dramatic results as soon as you try a medication.

You may still feel suicidal even after your anti-depressant starts to work

Be especially careful after your anti-depressant medication starts to work. You may still feel suicidal, and if you do, don't hesitate to seek help: contact your doctor, or call 911 or your local police or ambulance service, or go to a hospital emergency room.

If you experience any problems with, or side effects from, your medication, tell your doctor immediately so that he or she can take steps to help (change the dosage, try another medication, etc.)

Your doctor should tell you what the side effects are for an anti-depressant medication that he or she prescribes. If you suffer from these side effects, or have any other health problems while taking anti-depressant medication, tell your doctor promptly.

Agency-Based Counseling

Some agencies, especially larger ones, have in-house counseling or psychological units, sometimes using police surgeons or psychologists. Agency-based counseling can be very valuable, but there are several issues that must be addressed if they it is to be effective.

Confidentiality

Confidentiality is critical. If officers do not feel that what they tell counseling personnel is confidential, many will not seek help for themselves, and will not refer other officers for help. The agency must tell officers what the counseling program will and will not consider confidential, and the agency must maintain the confidentiality it promises.

Grief and Mouring

Shock

The death of someone close to you comes as a tremendous shock. When someone dies unexpectedly this shock is intensified and when someone takes their own life, or dies in a violent way, the shock can be particularly acute. Shock is common during the days and weeks immediately following a death. Some experience it more severely and for longer than others.

Numbness

Your mind only allows you to feel your loss slowly and following the death of someone you have been close to you may experience feelings of numbness. What has happened may seem unreal or dreamlike. The thought 'this can't really be happening' may recur. The numbness of early bereavement may itself be a source of distress and misunderstanding if one wonders, for example, why one cannot cry at the funeral. In fact, this numbness is only delaying emotional reactions and may be a help in getting through the practical arrangements. The 'protection' provided by shock gradually wears off and emotional pain begins.

Disbelief

It is natural to have difficulty believing what has happened. Where a death was untimely and sudden it is even harder to grasp that the loss is permanent and real. On one level it is possible to 'know' that a loved one has died. But on another, deeper level it may seem impossible to 'accept'. A large part of you will resist the knowledge that the person who has died is not going to be around any more. Confusion, panic and fear are common during this struggle between 'knowing' they have died and disbelief.

Searching

Numbness and shock tend to give way to an overwhelming sense of loss. Many bereaved people find themselves instinctively 'searching' for their loved one, even though they know that they are dead. This may involve calling their name, talking to their photographs, dreaming they are back or looking out for them amongst people in the street. This denial of a painful reality is a natural part of mourning. Realising that a death has really happened and is irreversible takes some time.

Denial is meeting your son on the street, seeing him from behind, the same shaped head, the identical droop of the shoulders, the swinging gait. Your leaping heart cries, "Oh, it's Mitch!". Some days, you'll walk into the house and 'feel' his presence in a room. You can 'see' that smile, 'hear' that laugh.

Anguish and pining

The understanding that a loved one is really dead brings

with it tremendous misery and sadness. As the loss begins to make itself felt, pining for the person who has died is common. Powerful and desperate longings - to see and touch them, to talk and be with them - may be felt. The intensity of emotions is often frightening and may leave the bereaved feeling devastated. Emotional pain is often accompanied by physical pain. It is common to go over and over what has happened, replaying things in your head or talking them through. The need to talk about a loved one, following their death, is part of the natural struggle to counteract their loss.

Physical and emotional stress

Losing someone close to you is a major source of stress. This stress may show itself in both physical and mental ways. Restlessness, sleeplessness and fatigue are common. You may also have bad dreams. Loss of memory and concentration are common. You may experience dizziness, palpitations, shakes, difficulty breathing, choking in the throat and chest. Intense emotional pain may be accompanied by physical pain. Sadness may feel like a pain within. Muscular tension may lead to headaches, neck and backaches. Loss of appetite, nausea and diarrhoea are also common and women's menstruation may be upset. Sexual interest may also be affected. The physical effects of shock usually pass with time.

The most common phrase heard from the newly bereaved is, "I feel like I'm going crazy". The pain and the accompanying emotions are so intense that it doesn't seem possible that a normal human being can experience them and still live. You may believe that you are going insane or at least on the verge of it but you are not. You are experiencing the normal physical and psychological reactions to deep loss.

Emotions during bereavement

Anger

Anger is a natural and common response to loss. It is rare to experience no anger during bereavement and, for some people, feelings of rage can be very intense. The protest 'Why me?' reflects a general sense of helplessness at the unfairness of life, as does anger at others for carrying on their lives as if nothing has happened. Anger may also have a more specific focus.

Intense feelings of blame may be directed towards other people - relatives, friends, doctors - who did not seem to help the person enough before their death. It is common to feel anger at oneself for 'failing' to prevent their death, blaming oneself for not doing more. Feelings of anger towards the person who has died are often particularly distressing and confusing. The bereaved may feel abandoned by them. Feelings of anger are at their most intense shortly after a death and tend to grow less with time.

One woman said after her son's death that she felt great anger at him for what he had done to her, her sister, her mother and family. She had often felt overwhelmed with murderous rage, rage at the world, at life, that it could be so unfair sometimes, and finally rage at her friends who she once loved and cared for...that they could not be there for her.

Guilt

Guilt or self-blame is also common during grief. Guilt may be felt about the death itself. It is extremely painful to accept that we were not able to prevent the death of a loved one or protect them. Feelings of responsibility are common and bereaved people often judge themselves harshly under these circumstances. Our relationships before the death are another common source of remorse. Sudden death interrupts close relationships without warning. Since our lives are not usually conducted as if every day might be our last, we assume there will always be the future to sort out tensions and arguments or to say the things that have been left unsaid. Regrets often take the form of 'If only's': 'If only I had done this' or 'If only I hadn't said that'. Guilt may also be aroused by what one feels or does not feel during bereavement (e.g. anger towards a dead person, inability to cry or show grief openly).

Occasionally a death may bring with it a sense of relief for those left behind, particularly if there had been a lot of unhappiness and suffering for everyone beforehand. This feeling may also cause intense guilt. Lastly, guilt may be felt for surviving - for being alive when they are dead. Another woman described her terrible feelings of guilt following her brother's death. Not one day had passed that she hadn't asked herself 'Why?'. Not one day had passed that she hadn't experienced the guilt, tidal waves of guilt that just seem to drag her under deeper and deeper. She agonised over whether they as a family could have done something that might have turned him around, that might have made him want to stay with them. Why she wondered did they say all those terrible things to each other while they were growing up? Or worse, why didn't she say all the things to him that she now wished she could?.

Despair

Feelings of despair are common during bereavement, once it is realised that despite all the pining and longing, a loved one will not be coming back. Relationships often suffer because despair is draining and saps interest in others. The bereaved may be left feeling both powerless and hopeless. Life may no longer seem to make sense or have meaning. Feelings of 'not giving a damn' about anything or anyone are common, as is indifference as to what happens to you. In the aftermath of a death suicidal feelings are not uncommon.

Fear

Fear is common in grief. Violent and confusing emotions, panic and nightmares may make grief a frightening experience. You may fear a similar event happening again. You may fear for yourself and those you love. You may fear 'losing control' or 'breaking down'.

The feelings of the newly bereaved have a lot in common with those of people suffering from depression. Like depression, grief can bring profound sadness and despair. Feelings of unreality are common. It may be hard to see a way forward. Grief interferes with sleep, concentration and appetite. For a bereaved person, these feelings are part of a natural response to a terrible loss. People who have been bereaved are likely to be more prone to sadness and depression for a number of years. For some, these feelings may be particularly severe and prolonged. When grief gives way to a longer lasting depression, further help may be needed.

Bereavement through suicide

The loss of someone you have been close to from any cause brings about intense grief and mourning. But the responses and emotions experienced by the bereaved following a suicide often differ from those felt after other types of death. The fact that a loved one's death appeared to involve an element of choice raises painful questions which deaths from natural or accidental causes do not. Bereavement by suicide is prolonged. Research suggests that the shock, social isolation and guilt are often greater than for other causes of death. The grieving process is characterised by agonising questioning and a search for some explanation for what has happened. Some people bereaved in this way feel a strong sense of abandonment and rejection. Whilst some of the special aspects of bereavement by suicide are described below, not all will be relevant to your own experience of grief.

Intense shock

The sense of shock and disbelief following a death of this kind may be very intense. A common and disturbing aspect of grief after suicide is recurring images of the death, even if this was not witnessed. The finding of the body may be another traumatic and indelible event. Going over and over the very frightening and painful images of the death, and the feelings these create, is a natural need at such a time.

Why?

Most newly bereaved people will ask 'why?'. However bereavement through suicide often involves a prolonged search for a reason or explanation for the tragedy. Many people bereaved by suicide eventually come to accept that they will never really know the reason why a loved one did what they did. During this search for explanations, different members of the same family may have very different ideas as to why a death happened. This may strain family relationships, particularly where an element of blame is involved.

Could it have been prevented?

It is common to go over and over how the death might have been prevented. Reliving what might have been done to save a loved one from suicide is a common experience of the bereaved. Everything can seem painfully obvious in retrospect. The 'what ifs' may seem endless: 'what if I had picked up on that warning comment or sign? What if I had not been away that weekend?'. Rewinding events, in one's mind or conversation, is a natural and necessary way of coping with what has happened. Research suggests those who have lost someone through suicide tend to suffer greater guilt, self-blame and self-questioning during bereavement than those who have been bereaved in some other way. While this is certainly not true for everyone, for some bereaved people feelings of guilt may be very difficult..

Rejection and abandonment

Those bereaved by suicide may experience a sense of

rejection. It is common to feel abandoned by someone who 'chose' to die. As one sister whose brother took his life recalled: "I was upset that he hadn't come to talk to us. I think we all went through anger at some point. You think : 'How could you do this to us?' ".

Suicidal fears and feelings

Despair is a natural part of the grieving process, but after the suicide of a loved one hopelessness may be combined with fear for one's own safety. Identification with someone who has taken their life can be deeply threatening to one's own sense of security. Those bereaved through suicide may suffer more anxiety than those bereaved in other ways and be more vulnerable to suicidal feelings of their own. The bereaved need extra reassurance after a suicide, which may also have been preceded by mental health problems.

Media Attention

For most bereaved people grief is a private matter. However when a loved one has died through suicide or other unexpected causes, it may attract public interest. The inquest that is demanded by law draws attention to the person who has died and to their close relatives and friends. The death and its circumstances may be reported by the media. Attention of this kind can be very stressful for bereaved relatives and friends, particularly where a death is reported in an insensitive or inaccurate manner.

Stigma and isolation

A mother writing about her son's death pointed out that

we've never been told what to say to someone who has had a suicide in the family. What she needed to hear was the same thing that might be said to anyone else who had experienced the death of someone close - "I'm truly sorry for your pain, and is there anything I can do? If you need to talk about it I'm a good listener. I've got a good shoulder to cry on." And she needed to know it was really meant. Everyone, she said, believes no one wants to talk about suicide, that it's best left undiscussed, that if you don't talk about it, it will be forgotten and will go away. For her nothing could be further from the truth.

Although social attitudes to suicide are changing, they may still limit the support that is available to the bereaved. The silence of others may reinforce feelings of stigma, shame and 'being different'. If others are embarrassed, uneasy and evasive about the way in which a loved one died, the bereaved may be left feeling intensely isolated. Opportunities to talk, remember and celebrate all aspects of a loved one's life and personality may be denied. A strong need to protect a loved one, and oneself, from the judgement of others may also be felt following suicide.

Needs of those bereaved through suicide

When a group of Canadian people bereaved by suicide were consulted about their needs, they felt they needed help and support to:

— get the suicide in perspective

— deal with family problems caused by the suicide

— feel better about themselves

— talk about the suicide

— obtain factual information about suicide and its effects

— have a safe place to express their feelings

— understand and deal with other people's reactions to suicide

— get advice on practical/social concerns.

Sources of support during bereavement

Each person's story will be different, and help must be offered in ways which recognise and support the uniqueness of each person's grieving.Not all those bereaved by suicide will want to seek support outside their close family and social network. Family and friends may provide all the support that is needed or a neighbour, teacher, priest or minister may step into a supportive role, listening and 'being there' whenever needed. But for others the death of a loved one will mean there is less support around. At a time when relatives and friends become absorbed in their own grief, usual sources of comfort and support may be diminished. For many the stress and trauma of grief means that additional help is needed. A range of professionals and non-professionals provide help for the bereaved. Possible sources of support are described below.

Bereavement organisations

Bereavement organisations offer support for the bereaved in the UK, both nationally and locally. Cruse provides help to the bereaved through its local branches, which offer individual counselling, social meetings and practical advice. This organisation publishes a newsletter for members and has an extensive list of books and leaflets. The Compassionate Friends is a self-help charity for parents who have suffered the loss of a child. Through local meetings and contacts it puts bereaved parents in touch with others in their area and promotes mutual support. As well as literature on bereavement, The Compassionate Friends publish newsletters for bereaved parents and one for siblings.

Self-help groups for the bereaved

Self-help groups for people bereaved through suicide provide the chance to meet and talk with others who have suffered a similar loss. This may be consoling in itself, given the feelings of those bereaved in this way that they are 'different'. Sharing feelings and experiences with others through group meetings can provide valuable reassurance. Unfortunately the existence of such groups is not widespread in the UK. Some local suicide bereavement groups do exist (see Useful Contacts section). The charity for bereaved parents, The Compassionate Friends, has a network for parents who have lost a child through suicide called Shadow of Suicide (SOS). Courses run by Cruse also bring together people with similar experiences.

General practitioners

Your general practitioner may be able to help you in a number of ways during bereavement: (i) by listening, talking and offering emotional support, (ii) by helping you with problems such as sleeplessness, anxiety or depression, prescribing drugs if necessary, (iii) by advising you on other sources of help and referring you to others e.g. counsellor, bereavement organisation, psychiatrist. Some GPs working in large group practices have counsellors at their surgeries.

The degree of emotional support offered by GPs during bereavement will vary from doctor to doctor. Some are more at ease talking about emotional issues with their patients than others. The bereaved tend to visit their doctor more often than usual in the months following a death. However, during a short appointment, it may not always be easy to start talking about all that has happened. One way around this may be to write to your doctor before your appointment, telling him or her of your loss and explaining a little of how you are feeling. Those bereaved through suicide report mixed responses from their GPs.

The prescribing of drugs during bereavement, for sleeplessness, anxiety or depression, is a particularly sensitive issue. Some people struggling with loss feel strongly that there are 'no pills for grief'. Others are relieved by medication which helps them to sleep or feel calmer. What seems clear is that the prescribing of pills should never be a 'substitute' for emotional support. If you wish for more time to talk things through, or longer term support, a counsellor may be able to help you. Counselling provides an opportunity to talk, in confidence, to someone experienced in listening to people in distress, who will not be shocked by your emotions. It may be a relief to talk to someone who is a stranger and who can provide a safe environment in which you may vent and explore your feelings.

Counselling needs to be distinguished from the kind of talking therapy that lasts for a long time and looks at the roots of present difficulties in past experiences (psychotherapy or psychoanalysis). Counselling will not force you to delve into the past. Instead it offers help with the emotional crisis and life changes you may currently be facing.

Church and religion

If you hold religious beliefs these may be a source of strength and support as you try to cope with your loss. Many people bereaved by suicide and other types of death find their local religious leader an invaluable source of help and often one through which they can obtain counselling as well as support. This source of support is usually open to everyone, not just people who have been religious throughout their lives.

The Samaritans

In UK, the Samaritans provide a national 24 hour confidential telephone service. They offer befriending and a listening ear to anyone who is feeling desperate or suicidal or is going through any sort of personal crisis including bereavement. They are available at all hours, every day of the year. The Samaritans have over 200 branches around the UK and during the day it is also possible to visit these branches to talk to someone in person. Your local branch of *The Samaritans* will be listed on the Emergency pages and under 'S' in the local telephone directory. When is it time to get help? Grief is painful and exhausting. It is not always easy to decide at what point it would be helpful to receive some outside support. Some reasons you might decide to seek extra help during bereavement are when you:

— continue to feel numb and empty some months after the death

— cannot sleep or suffer nightmares

— feel you cannot handle intense feelings or physical sensations such as exhaustion, confusion, anxiety or panic, chronic tension

— feel overwhelmed by the thoughts and feelings brought about by a loved one's death e.g. guilt, anger, rejection

— have no-one with whom to share your grief and feel the need to do so

— keep constantly active in order not to feel (e.g. working all the time)

— find you have been drinking or taking drugs to excess

— find you are worrying and thinking about suicide yourself

— feel afraid that those around you are vulnerable and not coping.

Use of alcohol and drugs

Some people bereaved by suicide or another form of death use harmful amounts of alcohol or take illicit drugs to relieve their feelings of sadness. While these may provide short term relief from painful feelings, they hinder the process of grieving and can themselves cause depression. They can also have other negative consequences for health. If you find yourself using alcohol or drugs in this way you are strongly encouraged to seek help. In the first instance it will usually be best to approach your GP. If the use of alcohol really gets out of hand you might consider approaching Alcoholics Anonymous for help. If one of your relatives gets into such difficulty Al-Anon is a very helpful source of advice and support.

A personal tragedy of this kind inevitably involves tremendous suffering for you and those close to you. Do remember that help is available if you feel this suffering is becoming too much for you to bear alone..

The length of time people take to mourn the loss of someone they have been close to varies very much from person to person. Some things such as sadness at the death and missing the lost person will probably never go away completely but the pain gets much less with time. An important part of the process of rebuilding life again seems to be accepting that the death really has happened and the person is not coming back. This can take a long time but helps people to get some of their very difficult feelings, such as anger and guilt, into perspective. Gradually the things which were good about the person when they were alive can start to be important, as well as their death. Many people find that although life is never the same again there does come a time when they can pick up the threads of their own lives and begin to enjoy living again. Although the loss of a friend or relative through suicide is always a terrible tragedy, some people find that they have been changed in positive ways by the experience. They may appreciate life more and be more attentive to others' feelings. Small reminders and memories can bring all the feelings of grief flooding back; anniversaries and birthdays can be particularly difficult times. When things seem very bleak it is important to live from day-to-day but remember that things will change in the future and that help is available if needed.

Mental Disorders

The strongest risk factors for attempted suicide include mood disorders or other mental disorders, comorbid substance abuse disorders, history of deliberate self-harm (DSH), and a history of suicide attempts. DSH refers to intentionally initiated acts of self-harm with a non-fatal outcome (including self-poisoning and self-injury). Suicide risk is assessed along a continuum ranging from suicidal ideation alone (relatively less severe) to suicidal ideation with a plan (more severe).

Suicidal ideation with a specific plan of action is associated with a significant risk for attempted suicide. Screening instruments are commonly used in specialty clinics and mental health settings. The test characteristics of most commonly-used screening instruments (Scale for Suicide Ideation [SSI], Scale for Suicide Ideation-Worst [SSI-W], and the Suicidal Ideation Questionnaire [SIQ]) have not been validated to assess suicide risk in primary care settings. There has been limited testing of the Symptom-Driven Diagnostic System for Primary Care (SDDS-PC) screening instrument in a primary care setting.

Although the incidence of suicide is low in the general population (0.01%), it was the 11th leading cause of death in the United States in 2000, with an age-adjusted rate of 10.6 per 100,000 people. Adolescents and the elderly are particularly at risk for suicide.

Risk factors for attempted suicide include mood disorders, comorbid substance abuse disorders, and a history of previous suicide attempts. Additional risk factors for attempted suicide in youth are aggressive or disruptive behavior and history of physical and sexual abuse.

Two-thirds of suicidal deaths occur on the first attempt, with higher completion rates in men than in women. Although men complete suicide more often than women, women attempt suicide more often than men. Between 3% and 5% of those who have had an episode of DSH die by suicide within 5 to 10 years. More than 90% of those who complete suicide have a psychiatric illness at the time of death, usually depression, alcohol abuse, or both. Almost 75% of suicides are completed by white males who have a 2-fold higher risk for suicide than do black males.

Native Americans are also at high risk for suicide. The evidence for the effectiveness of identification and treatment for suicide risk in the primary care setting. Because no direct evidence was found regarding the impact of screening on suicide attempts or completions, some studies examined the accuracy of screening tests and the efficacy of treatment on intermediate outcomes, such as reduced suicidal ideation, reduced severity of depression, reduced hopelessness, and improved level of functioning.

Little is known about screening instruments to assess suicide risk in primary care populations. Only 1 study of good quality evaluated a screening instrument, the 62-item SDDS-PC, for the identification of patients with psychiatric illnesses in the primary care setting. One of its items for assessing suicide risk, "feeling suicidal," was predictive of plans to attempt suicide with reasonable test characteristics. However, the study has not been replicated, nor has the specific item been tested independent of the longer instrument. Two studies of fair to poor quality evaluated the 21-item SSI and the SSI-W in adult psychiatric outpatients.

Patients who scored in the higher-risk category in the SSI and SSI-W were more likely to commit suicide than those who scored in the lower-risk category. The shortened 4-item Suicidal Ideation Questionnaire (SIQ-JR), developed to identify adolescents at risk for suicide in emergency room settings, has 98% sensitivity, 37% specificity, and a 55% positive predictive value.

In the U.S. Preventive Services Task Force (USPSTF) review, 33 randomized controlled trials addressed the effect of treatment of those patients with a history of suicide attempts on health outcomes and mortality. Thirty-one of these trials required recent DSH; the other 2 trials enrolled patients with borderline personality disorder. With respect to the outcomes on suicide attempts and completion, no statistically significant effects of interventions were found for which more than 1 study of the intervention had been performed.

However, some trends suggested incremental benefits from some interventions (in particular, problem-solving therapy for patients aged 15 or older). Of the interventions for which only 1 study was conducted, the most promising are dialectical behavior therapy (DBT) for adults with borderline personality disorder, interpersonal psychotherapy (IPT) for adults with DSH, and group therapy for younger adolescents with DSH. No studies were found that evaluated treatment for suicide risk in the geriatric population. The studies comprising the evidence base have 3 primary limitations: first, studies tend to be underpowered; second, standard care is poorly described and likely varies across multiple studies; and third, there is a lack of stratification based on age and age ranges are inconsistent across studies. This limits the ability of the USPSTF to draw meaningful conclusions about the effects of these interventions on future suicide attempts or suicides.

Several studies of fair quality evaluated the effect of treatment on the intermediate outcomes of suicidal ideation, depressive severity, hopelessness, and level of functioning in high-risk patients. No studies recruited patients from primary care settings. Improvements were described in patients with a history of DSH who participated in problem-solving therapy, and in women with borderline personality disorder who were treated using DBT, antidepressant therapy, cognitive behavioral counseling, and interpersonal psychotherapy. Among children aged 18 and younger, who had a history of attempted suicide, brief emergency crisis intervention involving mother and daughter decreased depressive symptoms at the 18-month follow-up.

No studies have directly addressed the harms of either screening or treatment of primary care patients at risk for suicide. Two studies found contradictory results regarding the harms of treatment interventions in a population of patients with a history of DSH compared with patients with no history of DSH.

Suicidal Thoughts

Suicidal behavior includes a child's stated or unstated thoughts about causing intentional selfinjury or death (suicidal ideation) and acts that cause intentional self-injury (suicide attempts) or death (suicide). Intent to cause harm to oneself is an essential ingredient in defining suicidal behavior. Intent may be explicit and strong, or it may be ambiguous and not well defined. Three categories of problems should prompt the primary care physician to probe further regarding suicidal risk:

1) psychiatric problems, depression, substance abuse, conduct problems, psychosis, past suicidal threats or behavior;
2) poor social adjustment (school failure, legal problems, social isolation, interpersonal conflict); and
3) family/environmental problems (interpersonal loss, abuse or neglect, runaway or homeless, family history of psychiatric disorder or suicide, exposure to suicide).

It is important for the physician to ask directly about suicidal ideation and plans. Routine clinical inquiry will not elicit these thoughts and concerns from an individual. Those with a specific plan and/or intent or specific risk factors should be considered at most risk. Among patients who present to primary care physicians, the following are indicative of high risk for suicidal behavior:

1) presenting complaint that involves a mental health problem;
2) recent history of physical or sexual assault;
3) history of suicidal behavior; and
4) those exposed to suicide through school or media.

Among those with chronic illness, suicidal ideation and behavior may be more common in those with diabetes and epilepsy. Suicide is the second leading cause of death among older adolescents. Between 12% and 25% of primary school and high school children have some form of suicidal ideation. The rate of suicide has tripled since the 1950s, which may be due to the increased availability and use of alcohol and firearms among youth. In addition, the rate of suicidal behavior has become much more common to the extent that 4% of high school students have made an attempt within the previous 12 months and 8% have made an attempt in their lifetime. Only one in eight suicide attempts is brought to the attention of a medical professional.

Among children and adolescents, the suicide rate and the rate of attempted suicide increase with age. The rate of completed suicide is much higher among males; however, the rate of attempted suicides is much higher among females. This higher rate of completed suicides among males is thought to be attributed to the more violent means utilized by males. The suicide rate is also much higher among whites than blacks, although the rates in both groups have increased. Native Americans have been reported to have a particularly high suicide rate. Socioeconomic status in general does not affect the rate of suicide, but a low status appears to be associated with higher rates of attempts. Uncertainty about sexual orientation also increases risk for suicide.

Outpatient Care

Suicide is the third-leading cause of death among adolescents in the United States. In the 1997 Youth Risk Behavior Survey, 21% of high school students reported suicidal ideation in the year preceding the survey, and 8% reported having made a suicide attempt... Additionally, suicidal behavior is consistently related to other problem behaviors, including depression, conduct problems, and school difficulties... The Problem of Treatment Noncompliance. The majority of adolescent suicide attempters are referred for outpatient mental health services.

However, follow-up studies of these adolescents have typically found very poor compliance with outpatient treatment... Improving Treatment Compliance. What can clinicians do to enhance the likelihood that adolescents will enter and complete a course of outpatient psychotherapy following a suicide attempt? Some promising systematized programs have been designed to enhance treatment compliance. Common features in such programs include making a highly specific referral (indicating time, place, and provider), reviewing expectations and misconceptions about therapy, directly addressing any resistance toward therapy, utilizing telephone reminders, and explicitly contracting with families about anticipated treatment length and/or goals... Psychotherapy Approaches.

Of the treatment approaches available to clinicians who treat adolescent suicide attempters, cognitive behavioral therapy is most frequently advocated because it is highly structured and can address the cognitive distortions so common among suicide attempters... Problem solving is another commonly advocated technique. Adolescent suicide attempters have been found to demonstrate significant deficits in problem solving, including limited flexibility, difficulty generating alternative solutions, and limited ability to identify positive consequences of potential solutions... Of course, a key component of any therapeutic intervention with these youth is the regular assessment of suicidal risk.

Common guidelines for managing risk include regular assessment of suicidal intent (both verbal and non-verbal indicators); negotiation (and re-negotiation) of a no-suicide contract; and provision of 24-hour emergency back-up.

Impulsivity, hopelessness, and anger should also be closely monitored, as these characteristics have been closely linked to suicidal behavior among adolescents. Clinicians should instruct parents to increase their level of supervision, to take all suicidal statements seriously, and to restrict access to any potentially lethal means, including both prescription and nonprescription medication, firearms and other weapons, toxic household chemicals, and motor vehicles.

Every year approximately 30,000 people in the United States and one million worldwide die as a result of suicide. Over the last 100 years, suicides have out-numbered homicides by at least 3:2. Concerned with high suicide rates, several federal agencies joined together and asked the Institute of Medicine to convene the Committee on Pathophysiology and Prevention of Adolescent and Adult Suicide to examine the state of the science base, gaps in our knowledge, strategies for prevention, and research designs for the study of suicide.

Suicidality can be treated. Pharmacotherapy and psychotherapy can be effective, particularly when used in combination. Continued contact with a health care provider has proven effective in reducing the risk of suicide, especially in the early weeks after discharge from a hospital. A number of prevention programs show promise for reducing incidences of suicide and suicidal behaviors. Programs that address risk and protective factors at multiple levels are likely to be most effective. Many of those who commit suicide visit a nonmental health clinician within the last month of their lives. This finding points to the important role primary care providers can play in identifying risk factors for suicide and in referring patients with suicidal intentions.

Because suicide is a low base-rate event, special efforts are needed to ensure collection of sufficient data to allow for meaningful analysis of risk factors and interventions. Currently, the reporting of suicide is non-uniform across jurisdictions, and the quality of data collected on suicide attempts is even more tenuous than that of completed suicides. Thus, improved surveillance is necessary. Clinical trials of psychoactive medications usually exclude participants at risk for suicide. Unfortunately, this practice precludes evaluation of treatments that could potentially improve outcomes for suicidal individuals. With appropriate safeguards, patients at risk for suicide can be safely and ethically included in clinical trials.

It is important to note that research has found that when news of suicide is prominently displayed in the media or suicide is addressed in a fictional television show or popular movie, there is a predictable increase in suicidal deaths among young people during the following weeks Sometimes, they take the form of "copy cat" suicides. Moreover, suicide clusters tend to occur more frequently than by chance alone. Thus, Shaffer, et al. advocate the need for "postvention" once a suicide by a student has occurred. Postvention refers to intervention conducted with survivors, school, or community once a suicide has occurred. They suggest that postvention can actually serve preventive functions by:

(a) providing structure for understanding death, thus alleviating some of the guilt and isolation experienced by family survivors,

(b) minimizing the scapegoating that can affect parents, teachers, the school, or particular peers, and

(c) reducing the likelihood of imitation either within the family or within the community or both.

4

Patterns of Suicide and Suicide Risk

Approximately two thirds of the suicides bore one of three risk factors before their death: a prior suicide attempt, mood disorder, and SAA (substance and alcohol abuse). Such statements in the suicide literature are very common. What is meant by a risk factor? Are people with one or more of these risk factors necessarily going to attempt suicide? Clearly not! 20% of the population may experience mood disorder during their lifetime, yet only a small number of these would attempt or complete suicide. Knowing that mood disorder is a risk factor, can we conclude that this condition is responsible for some suicides? While this conclusion is possible, the cause and effect relationship between the condition and the outcome of suicide is not known.

While knowing the risk factors for suicide may help the community to plan programmes to protect vulnerable people, with the current state of knowledge it is not possible to identify just which individuals will attempt or complete suicide.Students need to understand the concepts underlying the term "risk factor" and to apply this understanding to interpreting the statements about the risk factors of suicide and suicidal behaviour.

The term "risk factor" is defined as "an aspect of personal behaviour or lifestyle, an environmental exposure, or an inborn or inherited characteristic, which on the basis of epidemiological evidence is known to be associated with health related condition(s) considered important to prevent". The term can, however, be used fairly loosely to include any factor for which an association can be shown and is not restricted to those factors for which there is a clear causal link.

Examples of commonly known risk factors (and the conditions that they are associated with) are: tobacco smoking (lung cancer); sun baking (skin cancer); breathing environmental tobacco smoke (glue-ear); and family history of heart disease (heart disease) Many factors have been shown, in one or more studies, to be associated with suicide or with suicidal behaviour. Examples are: sex, depression, and previous suicide attempts. According to the above definition, most of these can be loosely called "risk factors".

The key words in the definition above definition are "known to be associated with". An association can be said to exist between the presence of a factor (X) and a certain condition (Y) when the probability of Y occurring depends in some way on X occurring. In determining whether an association is present, studies must be undertaken to examine the occurrence of the possible associated factors (the X's) and the condition Y. If a correlation is found to exist between factor X and condition Y, it is possible to say that "X is probably associated with Y". This statement reflects the fact that the determination of an association between X and Y is based on a statistical test which reveals that, within certain limits, an association is more likely than not.

Before jumping too quickly to the conclusion that an association does in fact exist, researchers need to make sure that every effort is made to rule out all other possible explanations. Important questions that need to be answered before one accepts the likelihood that an association has been determined are:

Could the association be a matter of mere chance?: Most studies will quote an estimate of the likelihood that a proposed association may be due to chance variability of either the factor or the condition or both. Note however that even if chance cannot be ruled out, one cannot definitely conclude the absence of an association, but only that it is not likely.

Could there have been some aspect of the study that has biased the results in such a way as to show an association when one does not actually exist?: For example there may have been some aspect of case selection which resulted in cases with factor X being more likely to be selected for the study. Perhaps there may have been some bias in the way questions were asked, which made it more likely that subjects would indicate the presence of factor X (or not). Were the data collected differently for people with factor X?

Have other explanations been eliminated?: There is always the possibility that X is associated with some other factor Z that is actually associated with the condition Y. The relationship between X and Y is therefore possibly coincidental. One can be more confident of the presence of an association (and therefore that some factor may be a risk factor) if:

— the degree of the association is strong;

— if there is a dose-response relationship between the factor and the condition (ie. the more X is present the more that Y is present);

— if there is a plausible (and testable) theoretical explanation underlying the association (it makes sense);and

— many different studies all show the same or similar association.

How are "risk" associations determined?

The determination that an association exists between certain factors and conditions such as suicide arise out of epidemiological studies of the condition. Initially, nothing may be known about the association.

Descriptive studies

Some studies are designed simply to determine if there is any pattern in the way a disease or condition occurs in the community. The condition itself and several other variables are measured and tests done to determine the presence or otherwise of a pattern. This may lead to the formulation of an hypothesis that one or more factors might be associated with the condition. One such method is the simple case study in which the case histories of many people with the condition are studied to determine whether they have any features in common.

In the early stages of a new condition this may be the only way to gain a fundamental understanding of the possible causes. Studies of cases of suicide have yielded a wealth of information concerning the psychological and biological condition of the cases, relationship patterns, life events as well as a range of other characteristics such as diet, alcohol consumption, education level etc. On the basis of these studies alone, conclusions can be made about the association between suicide and such broad characteristics as age, sex and race. This method is also used in studies of suicide attempters.

A correlation study design would on the other hand look at whole populations for the source of possible explanations. For example local government areas with differing suicide rates might be compared, looking for correlation between these rates and other variables such as level of employment, gross income, school attendance, type of industry, use of medical services etc. This type of study has been commonly used in sociological studies of the problem of suicide. In a cross-sectional survey, a sample of the whole population is surveyed to collect information about the presence or otherwise of the disease as well as other variables. An example is the National Health Survey in which information is collected about a respondent's physical and mental health as well as a range of known risk factors and a number of other variables such as demographic characteristics.

Characteristics of persons with the condition are compared to those without. These data represent a snapshot of the situation at a point in time. This method is obviously unsuitable for the study of suicide (dead persons cannot be sampled) but could be useful for studying suicidal behaviour. It has the particular advantage over a case study of being able to identify and collect data on those suicide attempters who do not present to hospital for treatment. For rare events, such as suicide and attempted suicide, cross-sectional designs have the disadvantage that very large numbers would need to be surveyed in order to give the study sufficient statistical power to make conclusions about any associations. This is overcome in a case control study where cases are identified in some way (usually from a health care setting) and their characteristics are compared to a suitable control group of people who do not have the condition.

Many studies of suicide and suicidal behaviour have used this methodology. The important feature of this type of study is that it is looking at the condition retrospectively, ie. after the condition has become apparent. By comparing the cases to controls, hypotheses can be formulated about what might have caused the condition to arise. As the central question is whether the frequency of certain characteristics in the group of cases is different from those in the control group, the most crucial aspect of this design is the source of and method for selecting the control group. "The crucial requirement is that they be comparable to the source population of the cases (eg. patients of a particular hospital) and that any exclusions or restrictions made in the identification of cases apply equally to the controls and vice versa".

In some suicide studies, cases of suicide are compared to in-patients who have attempted suicide, and/or to subjects drawn from the general community. In studies of suicide attempts, cases are often compared to in-patients who are in hospital for a different diagnosis or to subjects from the general community. It is sometimes the case that more than one control groups are used. In analysing reports of case-control studies students should give particular attention to how the controls were selected. Has the selection process used introduced any factors that could compromise a fair comparison between cases and controls. Has it reduced the capacity for the findings of the study to be generalised.

Another methodology that is sometimes used to study suicide and suicidal behaviour is the cohort study in which subjects are drawn from the whole population or from subsets of the whole population. For example, subjects might be drawn from different economic, religious or occupational groups. Data is collected at intervals over a number of years and the emergence of the condition over time is studied.

For the study of suicide and suicidal behaviour a number of different cohorts could be studied. Firstly one could study a birth cohort (the part of the population born during a certain time period) and periodically collect data about:

(a) the presence or otherwise of certain characteristics which are hypothesised to be associated with suicide or attempted suicide; and

(b) the incidence of these outcomes during the previous period.

Alternatively, one could recruit subjects from the patients who are admitted to hospital for a suicide attempt during a particular period as the cohort under study. Such studies are said to be longitudinal or prospective as at the outset, the eventual outcome (suicide or further suicidal behaviour) is not known. This design usually requires large numbers of subjects and data collection might be undertaken over a long period of time. Consequently, due to the expense involved, a reasonable hypothesis, would be needed to justify such an investment of resources. It should be noted that a cohort design can be used retrospectively, if there is a source of historical data that can be easily accessed and which is reliable. For example, the school absenteeism records of a cohort of sixteen-year-olds might be used to test an hypothesis between school attendance and suicidal ideation.

Intervention Studies

Deliberately varying the extent to which people are exposed to X and then testing to see if this has produced a change in Y can also test the association between a certain factor (X) and a condition (Y). In the field of suicide research, for example, one might (theoretically) undertake an experiment to see whether reducing exposure to guns in the home of teenagers would reduce the incidence of suicide events using guns. However, one would really need to have been already convinced of the association between the availability of guns and suicide events involving guns in order to undertake such an experiment. In reality experimental designs are used to test the efficacy of effectiveness of various strategies for reducing exposure to a known risk factor or for increasing exposure to a known preventive factor.

The term "risk" refers to the probability that something will occur (eg. people ask "What is the risk of rain over the weekend?"). If a factor, X, has been identified as a "risk factor" for a certain condition, one can refer to those people who have or are exposed to factor X as being "at risk". This means there is a higher probability that these people will experience condition Y. Just how much more likely they are to experience the condition (compared to those who do not have or are not exposed to X) is known as the "relative risk".

"If I am depressed and I learn that depression is a risk factor for suicide does this mean I am at risk? How much am I at risk?" Students reading this material may well have one or more of the characteristics or will have experienced some of the situations which are considered to be associated with a higher risk of suicide and may well ask themselves this question. How are statements of higher risk to be interpreted? Levels of higher risk are usually stated in terms of an "odds ratio" or an "aetiological fraction".

Odds Ratio is, as the term suggests, a ratio of two odds. Simplistically, if the odds that of someone with depression will suicide is compared to the odds that someone with no depression will suicide, we have an odds ratio. It gives a measure of how much more likely the depressed person will be to suicide compared to the non-depressed person. In Brent's case control study (using community controls) major depression is said to have an odds ratio of 27. This is interpreted as meaning that the chance of major depression being found among suicide victims is 27 times higher than the chance of major depression being found in the general community.

The aetiological fraction, is a term used for the proportion by which the incidence of a given condition would be reduced if the risk factor were to be eliminated. Patton and Burns quote an aetiological fraction of 0.29 to describe the relationship between depressive disorder and completed suicide in young males. This is interpreted as meaning that if this condition in males could be completely eliminated, the incidence of suicide would fall by 29%.

Risk Factors for Suicide

1. *Individual Risk Factors*

Male Sex	In Australia in 1995, rates of suicide in 15-24 year old males were four times higher than for females.
Living in a rural area	In Australia in 1995, rates of suicide for 15-24 year old males living in remote rural Australia are nearly twice those living in capital cities.
Aboriginality	Rates of suicide for 15-19 year old Aboriginal males are approximately four times higher than in non-Aboriginal youth.
Major Depression	A number of case control studies have consistently shown a strong association betweensuicide and major depression and this is considered as a very important risk factor.
Other affective disorder	Bipolar disorder has also been shown to be a significant risk factor for completed suicide.
Previous suicidal behaviour	One study using a prospective design has shown an elevated risk for suicide in young people who had attempted suicide.
Alcohol and substance abuse	One study shows that male adolescent suicide victims are six times more likely to have had reported history of alcohol abuse than community controls. Alcohol was the most common substance abused by suicide victims.
Stressful life events eg. Disciplinary crises or loss events	This factor is commonly shown to be associated with suicide.

Note that Patton reports that while psychopathology other than major depression and bipolar disorder has been shown to be associated with suicide, after account has been taken for major depression and other affective disorder, the association has not persisted. Antisocial behaviour, recklessness and other personality disorders had been identified as a possible risk factor in some studies. These were not reported because either the association did not hold up when adjustment was made for other factors or the authors had not made such adjustments, leaving any conclusion about the association an open question.

2. *Family Risk Factors*

Factor	Comment
Family behaviour problems	Trouble with the police is four times as common in the fathers of suicide victims compared to controls.
Not living in an intact family	Young people not living with an intact family of origin had a two-fold elevation in risk.
Poor communication between parents and children.	Poor communication between fathers and older victims held an almost 7 fold risk compared to controls.
Family history of suicidal behaviour	Suicide victims were five times more likely to have family member(s) who has suicidal behaviour.

3.*Community and peer Risk Factors*

Factor	Comment
Having access to lethal means	Studies undertaken in countries with a high level of gun

	ownership, show that living in a household where there is a gun is associated with a higher likelihood of suicide, and a higher likelihood that shooting was the method chosen.
Exposure to suicidal behaviour in the media	Evidence for an association between this factor and suicide has been shown by some studies but the evidence is inconsistent with other studies.

4. School/Work Environment

Factor	Comment
Academic Failure	Failing a grade has been shown to be associated seven times more common in white suicide victims in Nth America.
School disengagement	Suspension from school and dropping out were both strongly associated with suicide.
Unemployment, homelessness	Very high odds ratios have been shown for both not working and not being in school.

Risk Factors for Suicidal Behaviour

1. *Individual Risk Factors*

Factor	Comment
Sex	Most population studies have shown a greater proportion of females among suicide attempters. One hospital study showed a greater proportion of femalesamong people admitted to hospital for a serious suicide attempt.

Major Depression	This condition has been identified by a number of population studies to be strongly associated with suicidal behaviour, with one study showing aprogressive rise in risk with increase in depressive symptoms.
Anxiety	This condition has similarly been shown to be associated with suicidal behaviours.
Other affective disorder	Bipolar disorder has also been shown to be a significant risk factor for completed suicide.
Previous suicidal behaviour	One study found this to be the strongest predictor of future suicide attempts.
Alcohol and substanceabuse	Higher rates of frequent drinking, binge drinking, marijuana use, cocaine use and intravenous drug use has been found in suicide attempters in a population study.
Antisocial behaviour	While an association has been found in some studies there is some doubt due to no allowance being made for the effect of other factors.
Stressful life events eg.disciplinary crisesor lossevents	This factor has been shown to be independently associated with attempts.

2. *Family Risk Factors*

Factor	Comment
Family conflict and abuse	Child sexual abuse has been shown to be more common among suicide attempters (both males and females) than among controls.
Family cohesion	Each of the following have been

and management	shown to be associated with increased attempts: socioeconomic disadvantage; maternal deprivation; familial substance abuse; marital instability; childhood instability in schooling and place of residence.

3. *Community and peer Risk Factors*

Factor	Comment
Exposure to suicidal behaviour of peers	While some studies have shown an association between this factor and suicide atempts, otherstudies have not confirmed this.

4. *School/Work Environment*

Factor	Comment
Academic Failure	Having no formal qualifications has been associated with a six-fold increase in risk for medically serious suicide attempt.
Change of address	A recent change of address has been associated with a two-fold increase in risk for suicide attempt.

Emotional Distress Substance Abuse

Suicidal behaviour among adolescents has become an important concern in the United States. In a recent large-scale survey of high school students, 36% of adolescents reported experiencing suicidal ideation during the previous year, and 7% had made a suicide attempt in the previous year. Two factors that have been established as increasing the risk of suicide are depression and hopelessness.

Depression may set the stage for suicidal ideation, with more than half of depressed adolescents reporting frequent thoughts of death by suicide. Also, research has found that hopelessness and extreme pessimism about the future have a strong association with suicidal tendencies. Naturalistic follow-up studies have found that hopelessness is more closely related to death by suicide than is depression alone.

In addition to depression and hopelessness, alcohol consumption and alcohol dependence have been found to play important roles in suicidal behaviour. In a study of 913 adults with a primary diagnosis of alcoholism, 17% had previously attempted suicide. Furthermore, completed suicide is 120 times more prevalent among adult alcoholics than in the general population. Suicide is one of the more common means of violent death among adult alcoholics, with estimates suggesting that up to 18% of all alcoholics die by suicide. Both suicide and substance use may be seen as maladaptive attempts to escape from an intolerable situation.

Depression and substance abuse appear to be more lethal in combination than either factor is alone. Comorbid depression may play an important role in suicide among alcoholics. The majority of alcoholics who have died by suicide also had a comorbid mood disorder. In the general population, adults reporting depression with secondary alcohol abuse reported an increased risk of suicidal ideation or attempts when depressed. In a prospective follow-up study of 1312 patients treated for alcohol abuse, Berglund found higher rates of depressive symptoms in those patients who eventually died by suicide during the follow-up period.

Alcoholism may contribute to suicide risk even after controlling for depression. For example, among depressed patients, alcoholics report significantly higher suicidality than nonalcoholics. Furthermore, among adult suicide attempters, a diagnosis of alcoholism predicted eventual death by suicide. A recent study of adolescent girls, however, found that alcohol consumption did not increase the statistical ability to predict suicidal ideation beyond that obtained through information on depression severity and family problems.

Although few studies have examined the relationship between alcohol abuse and suicide among adolescents, the available evidence suggests that alcohol abuse may be particularly relevant to emotional distress and suicidal behaviour among the young. Among adolescents, the combination of substance abuse and mood disorder is strongly associated with risk of completed suicide.

In a recent study of 1050 adolescents, suicide attempts were closely related to the comorbid presence of depression and alcohol or drug abuse. Likewise, the rate of alcohol abuse has been found to be significantly higher in young adults (under age 30 versus over 30) who committed suicide. Among young men (aged 18 to 20 years), high alcohol consumption was positively correlated with suicide risk. In one study of young adults who died by suicide, 12 of 58 individuals who completed suicide were diagnosed with alcohol dependence. In addition, female adolescents who consume moderate to large amounts of alcohol are more likely to have severe and recurrent depression.

Alcohol abuse has been found to be related to the presence and severity of suicide attempts among adolescent psychiatric inpatients, with 15% to 33% of suicide completers having documented histories of substance abuse. Furthermore, a history of alcohol abuse is positively correlated with the number and lethality of suicidal acts. Suicide victims have been found more likely to have had major depression, comorbid substance abuse, and family history of depression and substance abuse.

Alcohol consumption at the time of the suicide attempt may be more important than the individual's long-term patterns of alcohol use. Alcohol intoxication is often observed immediately preceding both suicide attempts and suicide completions. Many adults who have died by suicide were reported to have talked about suicidal feelings only while drinking, and many adolescents who attempt suicide have been found to be intoxicated at the time of their attempt. The short-term effects of alcohol intoxication may prompt sudden, impulsive suicide attempts.

Alcohol use may be related to an increased risk of suicidal behaviour because the alcohol reduces inhibitions, making patients more likely to act on impulsive suicidal feelings. Thus one way that alcohol use can increase the risk of suicidal behaviour is by lowering the person's inhibitions at the time of the attempt, making it more likely that a person who has been thinking about suicide will act on these ideas. Substance abuse can increase suicide risk when alcohol is used as a maladaptive means of coping with depression. Furthermore, continued alcohol abuse is likely to induce or aggravate feelings of depression.

The onset of depression precedes the alcohol abuse for the majority of adolescents diagnosed with both depression and substance abuse. Thus the individual is likely to have been depressed and possibly suicidal for some time. When it becomes obvious to the individual that the alcohol has not helped to solve life's problems and has failed to reduce the depression, the individual may resort to attempting suicide.

The abuse of drugs other than alcohol has also been related to increased risk of suicide attempts, especially among the younger age groups. The rates of attempted suicide among drug abusers are comparable to those seen in alcoholic populations. Alcoholics who are also depressed or have attempted suicide are more likely to report the abuse of other drugs in addition to alcohol. The relationship between suicide and nonalcoholic drugs is especially prominent among the younger suicide victims.

In one study of 298 adolescent patients who abused drugs (predominantly marijuana, hashish, and alcohol), 67% of the patients reported suicidal ideation, and 30% admitted to at least one prior suicide attempt. Although substance misuse has been found to be an important predictor of adolescents and young adults who die by suicide, it can be difficult to separate the abuse of alcohol from other drugs. Alcohol continues to be the drug most widely used by adolescents.

Alcohol abuse plays a stronger role in suicide risk for males than females. The examination of gender differences in alcohol abuse may provide information about significant gender differences in suicidal behaviour. Gender differences play an important role in depression and suicide. Adolescent females are more likely than males to attempt suicide, whereas adolescent males are more likely than females to die by suicide. Among depressed outpatients, men are more likely than women to meet criteria for comorbid substance abuse problems.

While adolescent females may be more likely to admit to higher levels of depression, adolescent males may manifest their feelings of depression and loneliness through alcohol abuse. Family, twin, and adoption studies all suggest that genetic factors play an important role in the etiology of alcohol abuse. Their role in alcohol use among adolescents is also important. Individuals who abuse alcohol are more likely than controls to have at least one parent or another family member who is an alcoholic.

In addition, among individuals with a family history of alcoholism, the symptoms of alcohol dependence are more severe and typically begin earlier. The increased risk of alcohol abuse persists even when children of alcoholics are adopted away from their biological parents in infancy.

The evidence for the genetic transmission of alcohol abuse is stronger for men than women, at least for some forms of alcoholism. Among males, monozygotic twins have a higher concordance rate for alcohol abuse than do dizygotic twins. Age of onset may be an important factor in the heritability of alcoholism. Symptoms of alcoholism tend to begin 8 years earlier for males than females. Genetic factors have a stronger impact on the development of early-onset alcohol abuse among males. In addition, genetic evidence suggests that alcoholism and depression are separate disorders.

The role of emotional distress and substance abuse in adolescents who were hospitalized for psychiatric treatment following a suicide attempt. First, the study was designed to test the hypothesis that alcohol abuse would be associated with an increased risk of suicidal intent. Second, the results were examined to determine how alcohol abuse was related to specific dimensions of suicidal intent. It was expected that substance abuse would be related to higher seriousness of the attempt but to less planning and fewer precautions taken prior to the attempt. Third, it was expected that males and females would display different patterns of relationships between measures of alcohol abuse and emotional distress.

Specifically, males were expected to report higher levels of alcohol use, with ratings of alcohol use correlating with depression severity. In contrast, it was expected that females would report higher levels of depression and that their depression scores would not strongly correlate with alcohol use.

Suicide Risk for Same-sex attracted young people

Same-sex attracted young people (SSAY) are at greater risk of family conflict; rejection by family and friends particularly after 'coming-out'; attempted and successful suicide; mental illness; substance use and abuse; homelessness; victimisation at school; truanting and not completing school. The dynamics of family relationships often make it difficult for young people to feel safe about 'coming out' instead preferring to keep their feelings hidden which can result in suicide ideation and attempted suicide.

Mental health workers are continually engaging with families and the community and are therefore ideally positioned to take a lead role in improving outcomes for SSAY. By improving responsiveness to families using an affirmative and sensitive approach mental health workers can assist families gain confidence in dealing with same-sex attraction.

Persons identifying as homosexual are 2 to 7 times more likely than heterosexual comparison groups to attempt suicide; between 31 and 63% have attempted suicide, with those living in rural areas at higher risk. It has been estimated that SSAY are up to 6 times more likely to attempt suicided comprise 30% of all completed youth suicides.

In Victoria, the rates of suicide for males has increased fourfold since 1964 and the rates for females having doubled in the same period. An Australian study reported young gay men aged 14-24 years were 3.7 times more likely to attempt suicide, most commonly after self-identifying as gay but prior to having had a sexual experience. SSA young women are also more likely to attempt suicide than those identifying as heterosexual. In a New Zealand study of 561 lesbians, 53% had serious thoughts about suicide and 20% had attempted suicide, 80% of which were before the age of 25.

Reasons for increased rates of suicide among SSAY has been attributed to disapproval by family, peers and teachers and because of societal and internalised homophobia. "The risk is believed to be particularly high for adolescent gays at the time of acknowledging their sexual orientation, and exacerbated by being subjected to community violence, loss of friendship or family rejection".

While there appears to be a link between sexual orientation and suicide risk it should not be assumed that identifying as SSA is a mental illness or will lead to mental illness. Sexual orientation is not in itself a determinant of mental health. SSAY striving for acceptance among their peers are reluctant to identify as gay or lesbian for fear they will not be accepted within a heterosexual culture. Societal homophobia, internalised homophobia, fear of rejection and discrimination cause undue stress in the already stressful life stage of adolescence. This often results in invisibility and isolation, lowered self-esteem, depression, social withdrawal, less acceptance of self and sadly suicide ideation and attempted suicide. Repeated rejection, hostility and feelings of shame can undermine self-worth and self-efficacy and contribute to psychological distress.

Supportive family and friends, a sense of connectedness and opportunity to develop meaningful social and intimate relationships are vital to self-esteem and important determinants of mental health and wellbeing. For many gay men and lesbians support by friends and not family is associated with health, wellbeing and psychological adjustment. Friendship networks are as critical and influential as family of origin.

Victimisation, Harassment and Abuse

Significant risk factors for SSAY are victimisation, harassment and abuse due to their sexuality. In one study of SSAY, 46% had experienced abuse and 7% had experienced violence because of their sexuality. This abuse was most likely to be experienced at school (69%) with verbal abuse most commonly reported (65%). SSAY are also more likely to experience and witness violence than are those who identify as heterosexual.

Verbal and physical harassment by significant others including family and peers are associated with running away, school problems, conflict with the law, substance abuse, prostitution and suicide in SSAY, representing a real threat to wellbeing and in some cases physical survival. A critical time for SSAY is 'coming-out' which is associated with significant risks. 'Coming-out' is the recognition and acknowledgement of one's own sexual orientation and sexual identity as a positive aspect of oneself. It is a complex and can be a lifelong process. Rejection by family at this time is a major risk factor for SSAY.

SSAY who have come out often experience verbal and physical abuse by family members and acknowledge more suicide ideation than those who have not come out to their families. Sexual orientation is not caused by patterns of interaction of family of origin however, the capacity for families to adjust to the news will significantly impact on SSAY mental health outcomes.

Family Response

Initial family reactions to 'coming-out' can be negative but often improve overtime. Older parents, men, those with less education, and those with troubled parent/child relationships prior to disclosure are likely to respond negatively. The best predictor of outcome of 'coming-out' appears to be the quality of the prior relationship. The better the relationship the more positive the response. At the time of 'coming-out' SSAY report a range of family responses including pity, sorrow, sympathy, anger, worry and blame. In one study 25% of SSAY reported that their family had attempted to change their sexual orientation with psychotherapy, religion or forcing them to have heterosexual experiences. Many believed their parents are ashamed of them and express some degree of guilt in causing their child's sexuality.

Patterson describes the response by parents as a two-stage process. In the first stage the family struggles to understand and assimilate the new information. The family may deny the person is SSA or simply reject the young person. Some families will remain stuck in this stage. Over time many families move through a second stage during which the family reorganises and adjusts to accommodate the shift in the young person's identity. However, this may take a long period of time, even years. Some families may only in part move through this stage accepting some aspects while rejecting others - 'it's okay you're gay, but don't tell your grandmother' or 'it's okay the way you are but don't bring your boyfriend to family gatherings'.

Several factors may influence parents and family reactions. The family's cultural and ethnic background can be of influence, with homosexuality more acceptable in some cultures than others. Similarly, religious beliefs and practices may affect the level of acceptance. If another family member identifies as SSA there could be better understanding and acceptance, however this could also exacerbate a negative reaction and blaming of that relative. The younger the young person is at the time of disclosure the more a family may disregard the news, consider it just a phase or be more likely to attempt to change the sexual orientation through counselling and therapy.

SSAY who are supported by family, friends and peers are likely to be better able to cope with victimisation and the negative influence of stress on mental health and be more self-accepting and comfortable with their sexual orientation.

Affirmative and Sensitive Practice

Mental health practitioners have a vital role in supporting, reassuring and educating families coming to terms with a young person who identifies as SSA and can act as role models and raise awareness among peers and the community. Affirmative and sensitive practice can significantly influence outcomes for SSAY and their families. Affirmative practice values "lesbian, gay or bi-sexual identity as an equally positive experience and expression as heterosexual identity".

A practitioner must be comfortable with their own sexuality and feelings to be sensitive and helpful to young people and their families. It is important to question one's own attitudes, fears, feelings and prejudices toward SSAY and homosexuality and examine the reason for these attitudes and biases. Provide space and opportunities for the young person to explore feelings ensuring privacy and confidentiality. Affirmation rather than judgement of a young person's expressed feelings and sexual attraction will more likely gain trust and encourage a young person to share their feelings. Avoid overemphasis on sexual orientation, it may not be an issue for the young person.

Lesbian, gay, bi-sexual identity is one variation of a range of normal, natural and healthy sexual identities and sexual orientation may be irrelevant to the problem. A SSA young person may welcome support to approach their family about their sexual orientation but workers should never assume this role without the involvement and consent of the young person. While it is important to gain support of families not all families will respond favourably.

Practitioners should familiarise themselves with the language used by SSAY and avoid gender specific and 'heterosexually biased' questions. Similarly, practitioners should be mindful of how information about sexuality is reported, recorded and documented. Young people will be particularly worried about their parents and families finding out, but also concerned how the information may affect other workers response to them. Before sharing information with other workers check with the young person first.

SSAY are not a homogenous group. They come from many backgrounds and family contexts and as such should be treated with an individual approach and response. It should not be assumed how young people will choose to define themselves, that sexual attraction means being sexually active or that they are exclusively SSA. Stereotyping, either heterosexual or gay/lesbian, affects a practitioner's ability to be open to the potential a young person is SSA. Further it is not helpful to make comparisons with heterosexual population groups. While there are issues similar for all adolescents there are aspects of being SSA that are very different.

Families need clear and factual information to help them to gain better understanding of homosexuality. Families may need assistance to work through their own homophobia, gender stereotyping and expectations. Reassure parents that they are not responsible or the cause of their child's sexuality. Encourage families to question their basic assumptions and be aware of their own feelings about same-sex attraction, working toward their ability to identify, understand and work with their feelings. Sensitive and aware practitioners will seek out and provide positive images and role models to counter negative images in the media and the community. Focus on qualities and strengths of both the young person and their family.

5

Influence of Suicide

In the past decade suicide has become a serious health problem in our modern societies. The most recent surveys in the United States ranks suicide as the nineth leading cause of mortality, responsible for nearly 31,000 deaths. According to a recent World Health Organization report, suicide was found to be the cause of 1:8% of the world's 54 million deaths in 1998. The organization also reported that self-inflicted injuries including suicide accounted for about 814; 000 deaths in 2000. This translates into a global mortality rate of about 15:1 per 100; 000 or one death every 40 seconds. Accordingly, the World Health Organization has urged its member nations to address themselves to the growing problem of suicide.

In the majority of countries suicide rates are found to be higher among older adults than in any other age group. Owing to the current trend of a decreasing number of births in the industrialized world, suicide among the elderly is expected to become a major public health concern in the coming decades. Haas and Hendin estimated that there would be about 14; 000 suicide deaths in the United States in the 55 and over age group by the year 2020. Hence, since the release of the National Strategy for Suicide Prevention: Goals and Objectives for Action in May 2001by the Office of the Surgeon General of the United States, the prevention of suicide in later life has been a major concern of the United States.

Recently, after critically reviewing and evaluating the strength of the evidence from a number of empirical studies for whether correlates of suicide in each of three broad domains - mental health, physical health, and social factors - constitute risk factors for suicide in later life, Conwell et al. argued that affective disorder was the predominant risk factor for suicide in elders. Psychological autopsy studies from many countries also consistently show that more than 90% of suicide victims have one or more axis I major psychiatric disorder at the time of their deaths, and that the percentage for suicide victims over 65 is about 71% to 95%. This further suggests that affective disorder, in particular depression, is a predictive factor for self-injurious behaviour or suicide, especially among the older age groups. Thus, it is believed that the proportion of later life suicides would be dramatically reduced provided that affective illness was identified and treated effectively.

Although affective illness should be the leading target of suicide prevention efforts in the old age population, yet Conwell et al. emphasized that factors in other domains also played an important role in determining an individual's risk for suicide via their intricate interactions with the risk factor of affective illness. For instance, evidence shows that social support variables may both enhance and reduce the suicide risk in older adults, whilst physical illness is a contributing factor to the elevated risk for elderly suicide via depressive disorders. In fact, an individual's level of risk is in constant flux, reflecting the dynamic interaction of influences. Hence, a better understanding of those interactive effects will facilitate more precise preventive interventions.

Affective disorders are common in primary care practice, but often go undiagnosed and inadequately treated. According to the surveys, about 70% of older adults who committed suicide saw their primary care provider within 30 days of death, and more than one-third of older patients have visited their physician within a week. A recent national register-based study of all suicides in Denmark by Qin et al. also demonstrated that a history of hospitalization for psychiatric disorder was the prominent risk factor for suicide. Furthermore, risk was extremely high for those recently discharged from the hospital; about 27% to 37% have been in-patients. Thus, the evaluation of suicide risk by the depression and suicide feelings (life-weariness, death wishes, suicid). As the primary care setting is a significant venue for intervention, one important approach to late-life suicide prevention is, therefore, to optimize the ability of primary care providers to diagnose and treat late-life affective disorders and suicidality effectively.

Unfortunately, since many primary care providers taking care of the older people lack the knowledge or have unsophisticated psychiatry training, it is very difficult for the primary care providers to determine the degree of risk for suicide accurately. In spite of the large number of empirical studies available in the literature, there is no attempt in theoretically modelling the dynamics of an individual's level of risk for suicide yet. In particular, a dynamic model which can simulate the time evolution of an individual's level of risk for suicide and provide quantitative estimates of the probability of suicide risk is still lacking. A dynamic model will be essential to the design of effective suicide prevention strategies in the target population of older adults, especially in the primary care setting.

For instance, it helps to suggest on-going case management procedures for working with suicidal patients so as to offer timely and appropriately targeted recommendation according to a treatment alogrithm.

Gampling Related Suicide

There has been an unprecedented expansion of casino gaming throughout the United States in the 1990s as evidenced by the fact that,. including casinos on native lands, 24 of the 50 states have legalised casino gaming. This rapid explosion in the availability of gambling opportunities has seen problem gambling emerge as a major public health issue. Epidemiological surveys seeking public opinion suggest that the vast majority of gamblers enjoy gambling and do it for recreation and leisure. However, there is a small minority who gamble excessively relative to their available income and eventually meet psychiatric criteria for pathological gambling. In a meta-analytic review of prevalence studies, Shaffer, Hall and Vander Bilt estimated an adult population prevalence rate of 1.2% for pathological gamblers.

The adverse consequences of pathological gambling have been well documented and include financial pressures, depression, anxiety, marital discord, substance abuse, involvement in criminal activity and unemployment. These are known risk factors for suicide in the general population. Therefore it is not surprising that, given the psychosocial problems caused by excessive gambling, gambling counsellors and welfare organisations have also expressed concern that pathological gamblers represent a sub-population at increased risk for suicide.

Media reports linking suicide to excessive gambling losses have also drawn further community attention to this major public health issue. Two recent high-profile gambling-related suicides in Detroit may exemplify this matter. The first case happened on July 26, 2000, and involved a Detroit police officer who shot himself with his service revolver at a blackjack table in Detroit's Motor City casino. The officer had already lost almost $32,500 on the day when he made two additional trips to the ATM to withdraw $7,000 within 15 minutes. At face value it would appear the further loss of this amount led to his fatal decision to end his life. The second even more tragic case claimed not only gambler's life but those of his immediate family.

In this media report, a Detroit businessman shot himself after taking the lives of his wife and three young children. The apparent motive for the murder suicide was presumed to be accumulated gambling debts. A suicide note found near the deceased indicated the depth of distress experienced as a result of the impact caused by his impaired capacity to control his gambling urges. "There is nothing more destructive to life than gambling," he wrote, followed by a statement describing his sense of frustration at the level of government inaction to address the issue, "I wonder why there are government agencies to fight drugs and not gambling."

Recent clinical studies have reported elevated levels of suicidality in pathological gamblers ranging between 17% to 80% for suicidal ideation and 4% to 23% for attempts. In Blaszczynski and Farrell's detailed systematic evaluation of suicidal severity and intent, 40% of a sample of 85 treatment seeking pathological gamblers, were found to manifest clinically relevant suicidal ideation. There are few estimates of the rate of completed suicides among pathological gamblers but the Productivity Commission, using data extracted from the Victorian State Coroner's office case files, estimated that approximately 1.7% of 2,708 suicides in Australia during 1997 were gambling related.

Epidemiological surveys have attempted identify point-prevalence suicide rates and to compare differences in the distribution of these across gambling and non-gambling regional populations. These studies are predicated on the hypothesis that if gamblers are at a higher risk for suicide, suicide mortality rates should be differentially higher across gambling as compared to non-gambling regions or samples. In the Productivity Commission's survey of 3,498 randomly selected community members, 9.2% of respondents with a lifetime, and 4.4% with a twelve month history of problem gambling compared to 0% of non-regular gamblers seriously considered suicide. While these two epidemiological surveys have suggested a putative link between gambling and suicide within the community, the nature or strength of this relationship remains contentious with some researchers strongly arguing that no, or at best a weak, causal association exists between gambling and suicide.

Given that both gambling and suicide rates in the community are increasing and that both represent a major public health policy issue, it is important that empirical evidence derived from both epidemiological, mortality and clinical data sources is obtained to clarify the respective influence of gambling as a suicide risk factor.

Unfortunately, a search of the literature fails to uncover any series of systematic well-constructed studies of suicidality among pathological gamblers and of those that do exist, most are subject to major methodological flaws including the absence of clear criteria defining suicidality and clear guidelines to conclude the presence of a causal relationship between gambling and the completed suicide. In the majority of completed suicides, determining intent and the underlying motivation to suicide is frequently difficult and often based on limited indirect data and/or circumstantial evidence.

In one respect, the causal relationship can only be deduced with any degree of confidence by the presence of a suicide note that unambiguously describes a link between gambling-induced problems and the resultant suicide. But in the majority of instances such data is generally not available. For example, in a case series of 44 putative gambling-related suicides, only a quarter of the deceased left a note specifying the relationship of gambling to the suicide and even in several of those instances, reference was made to additional contributing factors.

Gambling may represent one among a multitude of interacting or independent variables that contribute to an individual's decision to suicide. With the presence of such comorbidity, the need for a psychological autopsy of suicide cases arises in order to disentangle the relative role that gambling-related problems played in the overall matrix of emotional distress and psychological pain underlying the decision-making process to commit suicide.

The Psychological Autopsy

Psychological autopsies are considered to be the core methodological strategy in suicide research that allows the construction of a detailed picture of the psychological state, emotional condition, behaviour and life circumstances of a deceased person in the immediate period prior to suicide. The fundamental purpose of a psychological autopsy is to obtain sufficient information on the deceased person's mental and physical health, personality, psychiatric illness, life events and relationships that may shed light on the reasons leading to the suicidal act. The primary sources of information upon which interpretations of reasons are made originate from coronial reports, medical records and information gleaned from interviews with key informants and collateral documents.

In order to fully understand the gambling-suicide causal relationship it is necessary to supplement a psychological autopsy by a consideration and analysis of the background socioeconomic status of the deceased in addition to relevant psychological and emotional factors. This is important if other explanatory factors independent of gambling accounting for the suicide are to be excluded. Such crucial socioeconomic factors include the educational background of suicide victims, social status, employment history, and occupational status at the time of the suicide. The interaction between social and psychological well-being has been long noted by psychologists and labour economists alike.

In particular, long-term unemployment can have a profound negative impact on self-esteem and mood. Loss of a job is more than just losing income. It affects self-respect, social status and the meaning and direction of life for the unemployed, particularly in the backdrop of economic hardship and recurrent unemployment. For example, findings by Marfels on resident suicides in the Las Vegas market indicate that there appears to be an over representation of unemployed persons among suicide victims of more than eight times the proportion among the resident population. The question remains as to the direction of causality: that is, does gambling lead to unemployment, unemployment to gambling or a synergistic relationship between the two that leads to the suicide.

The primary elements of suicide include the evidence of the deliberate self-infliction involving harm with the explicit intent of ending one's life. However, there are methodological problems encountered in determining and detecting actual suicides. Firstly, there are difficulties at times differentiating serious suicidal attempts from 'suicidal gestures' or 'attempts' where the underlying motivation is expressive of 'attention seeking' or a cry for assistance and where death occurs as an unintentional outcome.

Secondly, there are cases where suicides are erroneously classified as accidental deaths and consequently omitted from official records. For example, single vehicle motor accident fatalities exemplify the difficulty in differentiating an actual accident from a deliberate act of suicide. Such accidents are rarely classified as suicides although it is often argued that it is a common mode of suicide. In all cases, the accuracy of classification of deaths as suicidal is predicated on the reliability and validity of the investigative procedure undertaken in the process of the coroner's inquiry.

Gambling is defined as any activity that involves risking an item of value on the outcome of a chance event, and is generally applied to participation in any form of commercial gaming for recreational purposes. Stock market speculation generally falls outside this definition although it arguably meets such a definition. Similarly, professional gamblers are excluded on the basis that their gambling is to generate income.

Gambling-related problems are more generally difficult to identify and rely to a greater degree on subjective and, at times, value-laden judgments. Within clinical settings, 'problem' or 'pathological' gambling is diagnosed only where individuals exceed predetermined threshold scores on the South Oaks Gambling Screen or endorse five out of ten DSM-IV-TR criteria. In contrast and without specifying its necessary severity or nature, some more recent definitions have extended the concept by relying upon the presence of 'harm' as defining gambling-related problems and prefer the use of the term problem rather than pathological gambling to refer to such cases.

To determine the true number of gambling-related suicides requires accurate statistics on the total number of suicides occurring in a specified geographical region over a defined timeframe. While attractive, it is invalid to simply conclude that gambling was an instrumental cause of suicide on the basis that the deceased was known to have gambled, had accumulated debts or was found on a gambling premise.

To demonstrate causality, it is important to show that gambling was the predominant factor motivating the deceased to suicide. But in cases of completed suicide, the diagnosis of problem or pathological gambling is complicated by the fact that it can only be ascertained by reference to information derived from secondary sources or indirect evidence unless a health professional previously gave such a diagnosis in the context of help-seeking behaviour. Even here, though, the presence if a diagnosed gambling problem does not confirm its causative role in the final decision with other independent factors being more salient. Reliance is forced on information that is often of variable quality and reliability and derived from coronial investigations whose primary purpose, correctly, is to determine the nature of the death (accidental, natural causes or suicide) without regard to the inherent motivation or factors contributing to the decision.

Elements of Psychological Autopsy

The first step in the psychological autopsy procedure should be to obtain a comprehensive assessment of demographic and socioeconomic details with the aim of identifying predictive relative non-gambling risk factors for suicide, in addition to basic information regarding the deceased at time of death. A number of psychosocial variables have been identified as representing suicide factors. These include sex, psychiatric illness, affective disorders, unemployment, substance abuse, childhood history of abuse, marital breakdown, serious physical illness and loss of status , factors of often found in samples of pathological gamblers. Consequently, it is necessary to exclude the presence of comorbid conditions that could more parsimoniously explain the suicide.

A classification system is proposed based on the ranking of the quality of information regarding the presence of a gambling problem. The highest level of confidence suggesting a causal link can be obtained from direct statements contained in notes or audio recordings left by the deceased. The next order relates to information inferred indirectly from material contained in Coronial investigative reports, information produced by immediate family members, friends, neighbours and/or employers and additional valuable collateral data contained in financial statements.

By far the most convincing evidence linking gambling as a cause of suicide is the deceased person's explicit statement contained in a suicide note unambiguously confirming that problems related to gambling formed the primary motivation underlying the suicide. Typically, the gambler referred to acute states of psychic angst and depression suffering a sense of hopelessness in the face of a perceived insoluble predicament. Suicide, it is interpreted, is seen as the only solution that avoids intense personal embarrassment and/or loss of social status and self-esteem.

Indirect source of information

Information derived from key collateral informants and documentation that confirms the presence of a serious gambling problem in the absence of any serious co-morbid suicide risk factors unrelated to gambling. The presence of gambling behaviour needs to be confirmed through key informants' statements indicating a strong involvement in gambling behaviour. The frequency and duration of gambling activity and level of expenditure is used as an index of gambling involvement. Indications that gambling led to recurrent serious marital arguments, financial stresses characterised by insufficient funds to meet daily needs, regular repayments and purchases for special occasions such as birthdays, Christmas and holidays. Supplemental evidence in the form of bank statements highlighting regular ATM withdrawals from gambling venues represents further strong supportive documentation.

Further confirmatory evidence of the presence of gambling related problems can be derived from indications that the deceased sought counselling for problem gambling from health professionals or attendance at Gamblers Anonymous. Once sufficient evidence confirming a gambling problem has been accumulated, it is necessary to ascertain that no other ancillary condition was present that could more parsimoniously account for the suicidal act. Consequently, it is necessary to exclude cases where there is evidence of a chronic history of psychiatric illness such as schizophrenia or major depression that predates the onset of gambling behaviour, personality disorder known to be associated with elevated risk for self-harm such as borderline personality disorder, interpersonal problems characterised by a chronic history of social isolation and withdrawal from early childhood, evidence of childhood history of sexual or physical abuse and chronic substance abuse, the onset of which clearly emerges prior to a gambling.

While these factors may lead a person to seek emotional escape in gambling behaviour, they are capable of accounting for suicidal urges in their own right. Consequently, where a co-morbid condition is present, it cannot be concluded with any degree of certainty whether the gambling, the co-morbid condition or an interaction of the two were instrumental in causing the suicidal act.

The only exception is a current co-morbid depression. Here, evidence should be presented that points to the depression occurring after the onset of gambling and/or has increased in severity in association with gambling induced problems. Information derived from key collateral informants and documentation that confirms the presence of a serious gambling problem but in the presence of additional serious co-morbid suicide risk factors. Indications are that the deceased had a gambling problem.

However, the gambling problem occurred in the context of a major depression or psychosocial stresses such as a recent bereavement, interpersonal difficulties, loss of status, physical illness or substance abuse which may have had a catalytic or synergistic effect that in conjunction with the gambling, played a key role in precipitating the suicide. The direction of causality is difficult to determine but there is strong evidence to indicate that a gambling problem was present and on the balance of probability, represented a major risk factor.

Information derived from key collateral informants and documentation that confirms the presence of a serious gambling problem but there are sufficient indicators suggesting the probability of an additional serious co-morbid suicide risk factors unrelated to gambling, for example, schizophrenia. There must be substantive evidence from key informants and documented sources that a substantive gambling pattern of behaviour existed but not to a level considered to be problematic. Uncorroborated statements from key informants that the deceased participated in gambling behaviours that occasionally led to problems.

Where involvement in gambling was one element in a background history of extensive impulsive behaviours, non-gambling criminal activity, eating disorder, substance abuse, personality disorder (deliberate self-harm) and chronic social withdrawal and employment instability. Furthermore, a rating scale for determining cases of gambling-related suicides is suggested where the items are scored as absent, possible, probable or definite.

Suicide among Lesbian and Bisexual Youths

Studies of gay, lesbian, and bisexual youths have reported levels of attempted suicide ranging from 20% to 40%, with rates in some special subpopulations being even higher. The available evidence suggests that the relative risk for serious suicide attempts among gay and bisexual males is substantially greater than that among their heterosexual counterparts, but basic epidemiological research on suicidal behaviour in this population is both sparse in quantity and deficient in quality, plagued by methodological deficits, particularly with respect to sampling. In US, a study using National Health and Nutrition Examination Survey III data, Cochran and Mays recently found that 19. 3% of their sample of men who have sex with men (MSM) had attempted suicide, compared with 3. 6% of the men who had only female sexual partners.

However, the relatively small MSM sample resulted in wide confidence intervals (CIs) for that estimate in contrast to the narrower confidence intervals observed with the larger sample of men reporting sex with only females, and correlational analyses were limited to age, race/ethnicity, family income, lifetime prevalence of affective disorders, and lifetime prevalence of suicidal thoughts, wishes, plans, or actions.

Russell and Joyner, using data from the National Longitudinal Study of Adolescent Health, found higher rates of reported suicidal thoughts and attempts among adolescents reporting same-sex romantic attractions and romantic relationships than among adolescents not reporting such relationships, with this operationalization of sexual orientation having a significant effect above and beyond other adolescent suicide risk factors (such as depression, hopelessness, and prior victimization). Many studies examining determinants of suicidality specific to gay and bisexual men have focused on both developmental life transitions (e. g. , "coming out" or adopting an identity and sense of community based on one's sexuality) and social and cultural stressors (e. g. , stigmatization, victimization, pervasive antigay hostility).

The stresses related to anti-gay victimization and the "coming out" process (e. g. , loss of friends, antigay victimization) can be seen as having both a proximal and a distal relation to suicidality, similar to the immediate and long-term consequences of other traumatic events. First, they may provoke emotional distress sufficient to cause youths to contemplate suicide, and second, they may be linked to low self-esteem, substance abuse, and subsequent mood disorders that increase lifetime vulnerability to suicide.

Younger gay men, bisexual individuals, and lesbians appear more likely to both anticipate and experience stigmatization and victimization, which are linked to greater psychological distress. Societal stresses of being gay are not, however, buffered by support from usual sources (such as family), because many young adults have not disclosed their sexual orientation to family members or have encountered negative reactions to such disclosure. As a result of the alienation and anomie experienced by many gay, lesbian, and bisexual youths, conventional constraints against self-destructive behaviours (e. g. , social supports, problem-solving with others) may be weakened.

Furthermore, without the coping resources and psychological resilience of maturity, youths have an increased vulnerability to distress. Thus, we would anticipate that gay-related stressors (e. g. , experiences of antigay victimization, the sense of deviance and stigmatization prompted by an awareness of one's nonheterosexual orientation) and the paucity of psychological resources (characteristic of relative youth) are associated with greater vulnerability to suicidal behaviour.

A variety of models have been proposed to explain suicidal behaviour, including models that consider personality and social psychological constructs (e. g. , alienation vs sense of belonging, depression, stress and coping). We could not test such alternative models because of the limitations of the study data; however, we can explore associations between suicide attempts and several life-span developmental variables.

Most studies primarily used opportunistic samples, making it difficult to interpret the range of reported prevalence estimates. Large representative samples are needed to generalize prevalence data on suicidal intention and suicide attempts and to assess the effect of hypothetical determinants of increased suicidal risk.

Three items assessed lifetime suicidal ideation and behaviour: (1) Has there ever been a period of a week or more when you felt very sad, blue, or unhappy, like you wanted to die? (2) Have you ever made a plan for committing suicide? (3) Have you ever tried to take your own life? These are comparable to items used else- where, including the National Institute of Mental Health Epidemiologic Catchment Area study. Although these measures did not take into account the important factor of lethality, such self-report measures have been found to be valid and meaningful in other studies.

Number of suicide attempts and age at each attempt (up to 4 times) were assessed. To examine parasuicide (i. e. , attempted suicide) potentially related to gay or bisexual identity formation issues vs other issues, a cutpoint in age at attempt was defined for analyses. Current generations of gay and lesbian youths are coming out at earlier ages, with mean age at first disclosure by males being 16 years, compared with 23 to 28 years in earlier studies. Given (1) considerable interindividual variation in the timing of these events, (2) the fact that "coming out" is a process rather than a single discrete event, and (3) the sample's age range, a more inclusive age cut-point seemed appropriate. Analyses used a series of dichotomous variables: (1) any lifetime suicidal plan, (2) any lifetime suicide attempt, (3) any suicide attempt before age 25, and (4) any suicide attempt after age 24. Additionally, we examined age at first suicide attempt, number of lifetime suicide attempts, and number of suicide attempts before age 25.

Race/ethnicity (multiethnic respondents were assigned to the lowest prevalence category they reported), birth cohort (ages were grouped by decade, beginning with those who had turned age 25 by 1970, to stress the historical time frame of respondents' identity development), formal education, parental education (the higher of both parents), employment status (working full-time, working part-time, or not working-e. g. , unemployed, disabled, retired), and household income (in $20000 increments) were assessed.

Several studies have emphasized the contribution of disadvantageous childhood experiences to suicide risk ; thus, analyses included items on the occurrence of any parental alcohol or drug abuse, repeated (more than 1 occurrence of) interparental violence, and repeated childhood physical abuse by age 16. Childhood sexual abuse was operationalized as coercive sexual experiences before age 18 years. Logistic regression analyses comparing respondents who had attempted suicide by age of attempt coded no history of childhood sexual abuse when a suicide attempt preceded the age of reported sexual abuse.

The literature on suicidality among sexual-minority adolescents suggests that attempts are most frequent in the period between first awareness of same-sex feelings and first disclosure of sexual orientation to others. Various studies of gay men, lesbians, and bisexual individuals over the past 3 decades suggest a trend in which specific developmental milestones (e. g. , self-labelling as gay, lesbian, or bi-sexual; first homosexual sexual contact; disclosure to others) occur at earlier ages and are separated by briefer intervals. Early studies found that the mean time between first same-sex sexual relations and first self-disclosure as gay (or bisexual) among males was approximately 10 years, but more recent estimates have been closer to 4 years.

Therefore, in analyses, respondents were placed in one of these categories, based on the difference between age at first sexual experience and age at first suicide attempt (more than 5 years prior, 0-5 years prior, and after the attempt or never) in the anticipation that those whose suicide attempt was within 5 years of their first same-sex sexual experience were most likely to be in that vulnerable position of being aware of one's stigmatized identity but lacking social supports.

If respondents identified as gay or bisexual, they were asked the age at which they first told anyone. To be consistent with coding of first sexual experience with a male, the age at first disclosure was also converted to a relational score based on the difference between age at first disclosure and the age at the first suicide attempt with the same categories as above (more than 5 years prior, 0-5 years prior, and after the attempt or never). Repeated antigay harassment in adolescence. Respondents were asked about antigay harassment ("including being called names") before age 17; the initial categories were dichotomized so that "repeatedly harassed" meant 4 or more times.

Chi-square tests were used to examine univariate correlates of (1) ever having planned suicide and (2) ever having attempted suicide for categorical independent variables. Analysis of variance was used to examine the relationship of demographic characteristics (e. g. birth cohort, educational level) to mean number of suicide attempts and mean age at first attempt.

Two different multivariate logistic regression analyses are reported. The aim of the first was to predict lifetime occurrence or nonoccurrence of a suicide attempt based on only those independent variables that were temporally antecedent to the dependent variable. Identifying potential risk factors for suicidal behaviour in cross-sectional survey research is problematic because of questions of temporal sequencing.

The temporal confounding issue limited the number of variables examined as potential antecedents (excluding variables such as income, education, substance use, and depression) and limited the sample included in the first logistic regression. Because our measures of childhood traumas covered respondents' lives before age 17, the first regression analysis compared those who had never attempted suicide with those whose first or only attempt was after age 17. This process excluded 142 suicide attempters whose first or only attempt was before age 18.

The second logistic regression analysis was limited to respondents who had attempted suicide (n = 326) and examined independent variables that might differentiate between a first suicide attempt that occurred before age 25 and an attempt that occurred at or after age 25. The reported models include all variables that were statistically significant at P<. 10 on entry. Backward and forward stepwise regressions were run and compared for goodness of fit with the Hosmer-Lemeshow test. Because of the disproportionate sampling design, data had to be weighted, which precludes the assumption of a simple random sample. Weighting necessitates adjustment of both P values for evaluating χ^2 statistics and the estimated standard errors of means and obtained regression coefficients.

Studying Suicides

The most important method of studying suicides has for several decades been the psychological autopsy approach, by means of which detailed information on individuals who have died by suicide is collected through official records and inquiry of informants who knew the individual well. This approach has been the basis of many important and informative general studies of suicides in different parts of the world. It has also been utilized in similar studies of adolescents and young adults, elderly people; and subgroups defined in other ways, for example, by occupation.

Such studies can be relatively informative about certain characteristics of suicides, including socio demographic characteristics, methods used for suicide, psychiatric and personality disorders, problems and life events, and contacts with healthcare agencies. This approach has, however, several limitations, including distorted and biased recall of informants and lack of access to information about certain problems, especially those of a more personal nature.

On the other hand, studying survivors of suicide attempts which were very nearly fatal greatly extends the potential areas that can be studied because researchers have access to the living individuals themselves. Thus one can investigate:

— a broader range of contributory or risk factors;

— details of the suicidal process (e. g. , cognitive processes that lead up to the decision to try to commit suicide);

— the psychological characteristics of subjects, such as levels of depression and anxiety, hopelessness, self-esteem, impulsivity, aggressive feelings and behaviour; and

— biological characteristics, including functioning of neurotransmitter systems, genetic variations, and so forth.

This approach also allows follow-up of patients to investigate persistence or changes in characteristics. Thus trait and state phenomena can be distinguished. It also allows one to study response to treatments, occurrence of further suicidal behaviour and the circumstances and psychological process associated with it. This type of investigation provides a potentially very powerful means of developing our knowledge of the suicidal process and hence of potentially effective treatment and preventive strategies.

Serious Suicide Attempters and Suicides

The principle underlying this research strategy is the opportunity to study individuals who, through having come very close to suicide, share the characteristics of actual suicides, or are at least as similar to them as possible. Beautrais has recently reported the findings of a comparative study of young serious suicide attempters with young suicides in New Zealand. The distributions of many characteristics were very similar in the two samples. This applied to mood disorders, previous suicide attempts, prior outpatient and recent inpatient psychiatric treatment, low income, lack of formal educational qualifications, exposure to recent stressful events, and legal and work-related life events.

The suicides were, however, more likely to be male, which may reflect male preference for violent and hence more dangerous and likely-to-be-fatal methods of suicidal behaviour. They also tended to be somewhat older and were more likely to have a diagnosis of non-affective psychosis. On the other hand, the serious suicide attempters were more likely to have a diagnosis of anxiety disorder and to be socially isolated. Further comparative studies are required. They should take account of whether the criteria used to define a group of serious suicide attempters are an important influence on how similar the suicide attempters are to suicides.

An important question is how best to identify serious suicide attempters for studies of this kind. The approach chosen by the investigators in the Centres for Disease Control and Preventio (CDC) study was to rely on the physical danger and consequences of the suicidal acts, using the Self-inflicted Injury Severity Form. A broadly similar approach was used by Beautrais, Joyce, and Mulder in their study of young serious suicide attempters in New Zealand. This approach, however, fails to take account of suicidal intent; that is, how much an individual may have wanted to die at the time of the act. This is important because the physical out-come of an act of deliberate self-poisoning or self-injury may be greatly influenced by the means or methods that were available, and not necessarily correlate closely with intent.

To take an extreme example, if the most readily available means is a firearm or dangerous chemical substance, the outcome is likely to be fatal or near-fatal, although a substantial proportion of survivors of very serious attempts report having acted very impulsively, as found in the CDC study. On the other hand, the danger of, for example, an overdose of medication may, because of ignorance of what is and what is not dangerous, bear little relation to suicidal intent. Whether a person who takes an overdose of an antidepressant uses an SSRI, with consequent little danger of serious harm, or a tricyclic, with a far higher risk of death or of at least the necessity of intensive hospital care (e. g. , cardiac monitoring), is likely to depend entirely on what they have been prescribed rather than intent influencing selection according to perceived danger.

Then the person's degree of suicidal intent associated with the act would arguably be a better measure of how close in characteristics they might be to an actual suicide, rather than the physical consequences of the act. It could be thus argued that suicidal intent as well as physical danger should be used to define the group of subjects most closely related to suicides. Given that this type of research investigation is likely to become increasingly important and influential there is perhaps a need for an agreed definition that can be applied across studies and in different countries so as to ensure similarity of methodological approach and hence comparability of research findings.

Choice of Control Groups

The types of control groups which are chosen for research on dangerous suicide attempts is another extremely important consideration. The major determinant will be the nature of the exposure or risk factors that are being investigated. Thus, as in the CDC study, where researchers want to identify general risk factors, general population controls are required; and where the aim is to determine what factors influence the danger of an act of self-harm, then individuals who have carried out less dangerous acts of self-poisoning or self-injury are needed as controls.

On the other hand, where the aim is to examine risk and protective factors for suicidal behaviour in the presence of depressive disorders -which are found in the majority of suicide attempters-then depressed individuals who made serious suicide attempts will need to be compared with depressed individuals who do not have a history of suicidal behaviour. This may seem obvious, yet control groups are often chosen inappropriately. The above examples also illustrate how studies that aim to answer multiple questions are likely to be rather large, perhaps necessitating multicentre collaborative investigations.

There is no doubt that the CDC study is an important step forward in this field, in keeping with the similar initiative of Beautrais and colleagues in New Zealand. It is characterized by very careful and detailed examination of specific factors, using sophisticated statistical procedures. The researchers have examined a relevant range of variables, although, as is often the case with ground-breaking research, perhaps more questions are posed than answered by the findings.

The decision to focus on younger individuals (under 35 years) is reasonable given the specific issues regarding suicide in the young, especially the rising rates seen in many countries, and the relative paucity of information about risk factors for suicide in this age group. It is, nevertheless, important to remind ourselves that the findings cannot be generalized to older age groups, and that there may be differences even within the younger age group. Thus, for example, the social and clinical factors contributing to suicide in teenagers are likely to show differences from those relevant to suicide in people in their early thirties.

The overall size of the group of nearly lethal attempters (n = 153) is reasonable, although when subgroups are examined the power of the study seems less impressive. The group of less lethal attempters is rather small (n = 47) and there is rather limited statistical power where comparisons are made between the two groups. Having been involved in similar studies of suicide attempters, this commentator recognizes that obtaining large samples of appropriate subjects can present a formidable task.

The size and method of recruitment of the group of general population controls seem very reasonable. There is, however, as in many case-control studies using the psychological autopsy approach, the difficult issue that the rate of refusal and failure to respond is high and one does not know what bias this might introduce. For example, are individuals with psychiatric disorders more or less likely to agree to participate? This issue presents a significant challenge for this kind of research investigation.

The CDC study is cross-sectional, in the sense that subjects were only interviewed at one point in time. Because of this, the authors may have missed an important opportunity to examine, for example, whether certain characteristics (e. g. , alcohol consumption) persisted, the risk and nature of repeat episodes of self-harm, plus the patients 'responses to treatment. As noted above, a great strength of this type of study is the ability to study subjects over time rather than just on the basis of information gathered at one time-point.

One cannot but agree with the authors 'assertion of the need to look beyond mental illness in investigating risk and predictive factors related to suicidal behaviour. We now have extensive knowledge of the extent and nature of psychiatric disorders in completed suicides. The pressing questions are what other factors increase suicide risk, in the presence (or absence) of psychiatric disorders, and what factors can protect against or help reduce such risk. Recently there have been some other informative studies of young people that have begun to address these questions.

Some of the findings from the CDC study regarding factors that distinguish near-fatal suicide attempts from those of lesser lethality are perplexing. The association of prior suicide attempts with less lethal suicide attempts is not unexpected and in keeping with the results of a previous study. Within the repeater group will be patients who make several attempts of relatively low lethality, probably because the behaviour serves a purpose other than trying to achieve death. It is the association of greater depressed mood and hopelessness with less lethal suicide attempts rather than with near-fatal attempts that is surprising, especially as the opposite result with regard to depression was found in an earlier investigation.

Also, level of hopelessness has been shown to predict future suicide, although this finding was based on measurement of hopelessness often long before deaths occurred. The explanation given by the authors for this finding, namely that suicide attempters with higher levels of depression and hopelessness may have impaired ability to plan and carry out a suicide, seems inherently unlikely. While it is true that depression impairs problem-solving ability , the large weight of evidence linking actual suicide with depression and hopelessness strongly suggests that the associations should be in the other direction; i. e. , an association between more dangerous suicide attempts and depression and hopelessness. One wonders if the relatively small size and method of selection (inclusion irrespective of medical severity) of the control group of attempted suicide patients, plus the relatively low participation rate, could have contributed to this finding.

In terms of prevention of near-lethal suicidal behaviour, and, by extrapolation, completed suicide, the finding regarding previous suicide attempts is perhaps the most pertinent. One major element in most suicide prevention policies is improved management of suicide attempters. While the frequency of prior suicide attempts in the near-lethal suicide at-tempter group (47.4%) means that this is important, the fact that more than half the individuals in this group had not made prior attempts means that preventive efforts must also be targeted at earlier stages in the suicidal process, as well as at reducing availability of dangerous means for suicide.

In the CDC study, alcohol consumption and abuse have been examined in considerable detail, with a focus on three areas -alcohol dependency, usual drinking patterns, and drinking immediately prior to the suicide attempt. The findings confirm the importance of alcohol dependency as a risk factor for suicidal behaviour. More detailed inquiry of the suicide attempters regarding how they, in retrospect, perceived the role of their alcohol consumption immediately preceding the attempts could have been informative. Such inquiry might, for example, have established the extent of importance of the potentially disinhibiting effect of alcohol in relation to suicidal impulses, or the extent to which drinking contributed to or compounded the individuals ' life problems.

The association between geographical mobility, a known risk factor for suicidal behaviour, and risk of a near-lethal suicide attempt has been studied in a particularly elegant way in the CDC study, with careful control for certain potential confounding factors, namely gender, depression, and alcohol dependency. The dose-response associations of increasing risk with increases in the number of moves, distance moved, and difficulty of staying in touch with friends and family, strongly supports a specific contribution of geographic mobility and social isolation to risk of serious suicide attempts. The number of moves in the 12 months before the suicide attempts emerged as the key mobility variable associated with risk.

Impulsive Suicide Attempts

One cannot dispute that the cut-off point for impulsive suicide attempts in the CDC study of less than 5 minutes between making the decision to attempt suicide and carrying out the actual act represents extreme impulsivity.

The findings that more impulsive suicide attempts were associated with male sex and a history of fighting is unsurprising given the link between impulsivity and aggression. Inclusion of a more general measure of impulsivity than the three questions which were asked (fighting, quitting job, multiple sex partners) would have allowed the potential association of impulsivity with nature of suicide attempt to have been investigated further. The absence of an association of impulsive attempts with alcohol consumption beforehand is perhaps surprising given the well-recognized disinhibiting effects of alcohol.

Perhaps the most important implication of a highly impulsive suicide attempt is that it is most likely to involve a method of suicidal behaviour that is immediately to hand. This is the situation in which a policy of limiting availability of dangerous means for suicidal actions is most likely to be effective. It has clear relevance to limiting availability of means such as firearms, dangerous medicines, and toxic substances such as pesticides and insecticides.

6

Suicide Among Teens, Adults and Elderly

Since the 1950s, suicide rates have increased dramatically among young people in all over the world. Suicide is the third leading cause of death of young people between the ages of 15 and 24 in the U.S., and the second leading cause in Canada. Although official suicide rates are much lower for children under 15, suicidal behavior has been reported even in very young children. It is generally accepted that many suicides are unreported or misreported as accidents or death due to undetermined causes (particularly for young children). It has been estimated that the actual number of suicides may be two to three times greater than official statistics indicate.

The presence of a psychiatric disorder—particularly a mood disorder such as depression or bipolar illness, a conduct disorder, or a psychosis—contributes to the likelihood of suicide. Depression often exists in conjunction with other mental disorders or with other long-lasting social or behavioral problems. However, not all students with depression or other psychiatric disorders are suicidal.

Very little information is available regarding the prevalence of depression or suicide in students who receive special education services, although relationships between cognitive deficits and depression and between diminished problem-solving abilities and suicidal behavior have been noted. Medical problems have also been associated with depression and suicide. Estimates of the prevalence of depression or symptoms of depression among children and youth with learning or behavior problems tend to be higher than those for the general population.

Children with symptoms of depression, particularly gifted children or children who do not also exhibit symptoms of another disorder, may be overlooked in the school referral process for special education services. Researchers have attempted to identify situations, experiences, or characteristics that contribute to the likelihood that a child will complete a suicide. When a child has more than one of these factors, the risk of suicide is increased. In addition to mental illness and behavior disorders, suicide has been associated with demographic factors, such as being between the ages of 15 and 24, being white or male, or having a history of attempted suicide.

Psychosocial conditions, such as parental loss, family disruption, exposure to suicide, unwanted pregnancy, and particularly, having a relative who has committed suicide are additional factors. Certain biological conditions have also been associated with suicide; these include perinatal factors, decreases in levels of serotonin, and decreases in the secretion of growth hormone, among others.

The American Association of Suicidology has developed guidelines for the media, aimed at reducing the contagious effects of suicide reports. They recommend that the press avoid providing specific details of the method, romanticization of the suicide, descriptions of suicide as unexplainable, and simplistic reasons for the suicide. Further, news stories about suicide should not be printed on the front page, the word suicide should not be in the headline, and a picture of the person who committed suicide should not be printed.

Suicidal ideas, threats, and attempts often precede a suicide. The most commonly cited warnings of potential suicide include (a) extreme changes in behavior, (b) a previous suicide attempt, (c) a suicidal threat or statement, and (d) signs of depression. Young children who have depression may have physical complaints, be agitated, or hear imaginary voices. Adolescents may have school difficulties, may withdraw from social activities, have negative or antisocial behavior, or may use alcohol or other drugs. They may display increased emotionality, and their moods may be restless, grouchy, aggressive, or sulky. They may not pay attention to their personal appearance. They may refuse to cooperate in family ventures or want to leave home. They may feel that they are not understood or that they are not approved of, or they may be very sensitive to rejection in love relationships.

What Can Educators Do?

The primary role of all school personnel is to detect the signs of depression and potential suicide, to make immediate referrals to the contact person within the school, to notify parents, to secure assistance from school and community resources, and to assist as members of the support team in follow-up activity after a suicide threat or attempt. Special educators should be aware that many exceptional students, particularly those with emotional or behavioral disorders, may be depressed or potentially suicidal, and also that many depressed or suicidal youngsters are not referred for special education services. Discussions with students should stress the individuals and agencies that are available to help students and the steps they can take in seeking help for themselves, their friends, and their families in case of emergencies.

When a classroom teacher notices changes in a student that may be an indicator of suicidal behavior, immediate action is crucial. Teachers and other school personnel who detect signs of depression or potential suicide in a student must immediately notify the school contact person, who will in turn notify the parents and other appropriate individuals in the school or community. The student should be kept under close supervision and must not be left alone. It is important to let the student know that adults in the school are concerned about his or her welfare. Students who are depressed or suicidal may misinterpret uncertainty or failure to respond as a lack of caring.

One course of action for students who show signs of depression or potential suicide is referral for special education assessment. A special education teacher can provide a safe, structured, and positive classroom environment and an appropriate, effective educational program. Classroom behavior management systems that emphasize support, encouragement, gains, and rewards rather than punishment should be implemented. The individualized education program (IEP) of a student with symptoms of depression or suicidal behavior should include goals and objectives related to the alleviation of risk factors.

School assessments should be regarded as additional to, rather than a substitute for, an assessment by a mental health professional. Authorities have often suggested that evaluation for suicide potential should be included in the diagnostic procedure for any child referred for any reason to a physician or psychiatrist. The assessment process provides a means of consulting with parents and other school professionals and an opportunity to assess the risk factors present in the student's life. Alleviation of the risk factors should be goals on the student's IEP. The involvement of the family as part of the school program for depressed and potentially suicidal youngsters is extremely important.

School psychologists are important members of the IEP team for depressed or suicidal children. Assessment instruments suitable for use by school psychologists who have received specific training are available. Many clinicians feel that a battery of screening and assessment instruments, including a variety of assessment techniques such as interviews, checklists, questionnaires, and inventories is required for an accurate assessment of depression and suicidal risk. The role of the school psychologist may also include crisis intervention and treatment within the school. If these responsibilities are part of the school psychologist's role, they should be included in the job description, and the psychologist should carry liability insurance.

Components of an Effective School Program

Many school suicide prevention programs have not been evaluated for efficacy and safety. Researchers have questioned the effectiveness of curricular programs, and some research suggests that such programs may actually increase the risk for students who have attempted suicide. They recommended instead that schools concentrate on providing individual assistance to students who are most at risk. Schools should exercise caution in developing a plan for suicide prevention, but a written and approved plan must be developed.

Each school plan should be developed by the district's own committee and should be a team effort by all individuals, groups, and agencies that may be affected by its implementation. A comprehensive program will include procedures related to all three levels of prevention—for the aftermath of a suicide crisis (tertiary prevention), for dealing with suicide attempts, threats, and ideation, (secondary prevention), and for the enhancement of mental health (primary prevention).

The full continuum of special education services—ranging from counseling, special materials, and specialized instruction within the regular school program to short- and long-term residential placements—is an essential component of the intervention plan. It is advisable to seek legal counsel regarding the plan to address issues of liability. A comprehensive plan would include the following:

— Crisis teams at the school and district levels as well as a community crisis team or network of professionals.

— A contact person, such as the school counselor, who is designated to maintain communication among teachers, students, parents, and community treatment providers.

— Case management.

— Procedures for documenting referrals, notifying parents and working with depressed or suicidal students.

— Policies and procedures that clearly delineate the appropriate steps to follow in the event of suicidal behavior and the responsibilities of the various school personnel in carrying out the plan.

— Training for teachers and other school personnel.

— Provision of positive information to students about the symptoms of depression and suicidal behavior, resources available in the school and community, and procedures for referring themselves or others to these services.

Suicide accounts for 2% of all deaths in the U.S. but 15% of adolescent deaths. That means approximately 2000 adolescents commit suicide each year. Relative to other Southern states, Florida tends to have a higher than average suicide rate, a statistic that is also complicated by Florida's relatively low rate of adequate health insurance coverage and relatively high rate of alcohol consumption. Suicide attempts are approximately seven times more common than completed events. As with adults the vast majority (75-90%) of all adolescent suicide attempts were by drug overdose.

Also as with adults females account for 75% of the attempts, while males account for 75% of actual suicides. Approximately two of three High School students have had some degree of suicidal ideation. Approximately only one in ten adolescents will make at least one attempt. While many studies have provided us with a wealth of statistical data, and while clinical psychologists and other mental health providers see many individuals in suicidal crisis, completed suicide remains difficult to predict due to the fact that it remains a relatively rare event in the larger context of the many people considered to be at risk.

Many of the factors used as general suicide predictors are factors which would raise concern about the child or adolescent in a broader psychological context. Medical personal and parents of children with chronic illness should note that as has been found with adults, chronic physical illness is an important variable in the background of adolescent suicide attempters. While most psychologists and other professionals agree that predicting suicide is difficulty, many agree that depression of all subtypes and the emergence of helplessness and hopelessness are associated with increased risk. As with much behavior, the best predictor is the past.

Previous history of attempts, communication of intent and significant negative life events are particularly important. Persisting suicidal ideation even for a few days warrants attention. Particular concern arises when coping skills become overwhelmed, there is a loss or withdrawal from sources of support, and thinking becomes irrational or very rigid. Many people can easily understand that depression may carry an increased suicide risk. While studies have estimated that 83% of suicides were depressed, it is equally important to remember that the majority of depressed adolescents and adults are not suicidal.

Parents and even physicians and other professionals may tend to underestimate the risk posed by otherwise very impulsive children or adolescents with more general adjustment difficulties and a history of risk-taking behavior. Since many suicidal acts are impulsive, adolescents may tend to use whatever means are easily available. Parents with concerns about a depressed or suicidal child or teen should secure or remove firearms from the home, and lock medication and hazardous substances. Psychologists and other mental health professionals are aware that there may be high risk times in which individuals with elevated suicide risk should be more closely monitored. These involve times where there are significant losses. For children and adolescents these could involve loss of a family member, close friend, parental divorce, a breakup of an amorous relationship, or moves to different schools or homes.

Psychological events and real or imagined failures which involve embarrassment, shame or humiliation must also be attended to. Psychologists and others have studied several risk factors for suicide in adolescents and young adults. Acute or chronic alcohol or drug abuse is associated with elevated risk. Some have reported that approximately a third of adolescents who commit suicide are intoxicated at the time. Parental alcohol orsubstance abuse problems has also been demonstrated to be a factor in at-risk children and adolescents.

Certain psychiatric disorders such as mood disorders, schizophrenia and Borderline Personality Disorder have been associated with increased risk. Children and adolescents with aggressive or impulsive patterns of behavior or with conduct disorders are at risk. Family psychiatric disorders are also relevant. Emotional states associated with adolescent suicide include depression, hopelessness and anger. These are associated with psychiatric admission, future attempts, and more distress.

History of family problems and family violence is often found in the histories of suicidal adolescents. Abused children have higher rates even when compared to neglected children. Sexual abuse has also been noted in the history adolescents seen in hospital emergency rooms for suicide attempts. Death of a family member has long been associated with grief and depression. Recent deaths of family members or other psychologically important individuals also place children and adolescents at risk.

Psychological losses or separations such as those caused by divorce, changes in school, or moves can also be contributors. Impaired social skills and impaired peer relationships are associated with suicidal adolescents. Though a substantial proportion psychiatrically hospitalized adolescents having made suicide attempts may describe themselves as loners, studies concerning peer relationships has not always found a consistent relationship. Being the friend or family member of a suicide victim places individuals at particularly high risk.

Adolescent attempters are more likely those with ideation or and non-suicidal students to know another peer who had attempted suicide. This has prompted many schools to pro-actively conduct crisis management sessions and screening when a student commits suicide. Copy-cat suicides are not a new phenomenon and increased rates of suicide have sometimes been associated with publicized suicides. As with much of behavior in general, the best single predictor is a previous suicide attempt. Estimates have suggested that as many as 40% of adolescents making a prior attempt will try again. Even more alarming is that one of 20 individuals with a history of more than one attempt will succeed in a suicide attempt.

Repeat attempters are likely to have had school difficulties, serious life stressors as well as elevated levels of anger and depression. Older adolescent males with chronic conduct problems and poor impulse control make up a large proportion of these repeat attempters. Humiliation and frustration suffered by some adolescents struggling with conflicts about their sexual development or orientation may sometimes precipitate suicidal behavior.

Short term predictors often involve experiences that are experienced as shameful or humiliating by the child or adolescent. Arrests, perceived failures at school or work, rejection, interpersonal conflict with a romantic partner, or conflict with a parent are common experiences that can sometimes trigger distress and attempts. It is largely agreed upon that the emergence of hopelessness often precedes attempts.

Ready access to lethal means is particularly associated with completed attempts. Only approximately one of four suicides demonstrate any significant prior planning. This means reducing access to lethal means is very important particularly when there is a child or adolescent identified to be otherwise at risk in the home. Medications used are usually those easily found in the home. The rate of suicide by firearms since 1950 has increased three times faster than other methods.

Psychologists have studied the thinking patterns of at-risk adolescents. Difficulties in problem solving, general impulsiveness, negative expectation about rewards and consequence, a persistent negative self-image, treating oneself as an object, and hopelessness are some of the characteristics that have been described. It is important to note that 80% of attempts and completions are preceded by warning. Though the majority of threats are not followed by attempt parents and professionals must take warnings seriously.

Sometimes the only warning is given to peers. Adolescents should be encouraged to report warnings.

Unfortunately, it is likely only half of all adolescent suicide attempters receive any form of psychotherapy. Sometimes, parental lack of cooperation or denial of the seriousness of the attempts serve as obstacles to adolescents receiving appropriate treatment. Parental attitudes about receiving psychological or mental health assistance and family background often determine which children get opportunities for help.

Research has indicated that compliance with follow-up improves when appointments are made for the adolescent or family with a specific provider as opposed to simply giving the caller a name and telephone number. Dissatisfaction with previous psychiatric treatment, complicated managed care procedures, and managed care restriction of provider choice may also present hurdles to seeking and following up for treatment.

Since early treatment of depression and other mental health conditions and careful follow-up of at-risk children and adolescents is the best prevention, particularly stringent managed care mental health benefits for adolescents and children is problematic. Health care reform regarding children's mental health benefits continues to part of national and state debates. Significant progress can be made in reducing childhood and adolescent suicide may depend upon mental illness being treated on a par with other life-threatening medical disorders and efforts to reduce barriers to direct access to mental health care.

Preventative measures such as education of emergency room personnel, runaway shelters, pediatricians, and mental health care providers are needed. Parent should educate themselves or ask their doctors about signs and symptoms of childhood and adolescent depression and should become familiar with community resources.

With Increasing Frequency, the estates and families of students who have committed suicide are suing school systems. In most instances, such cases are dismissed before reaching trial. This cause of action is not without teeth, however. Under both survival statutes and wrongful death statutes, school boards have been forced to pay monetary damages.

The death of a child is a tragedy for the child's family, friends, and community. The suicide of a child causes still greater damage. Two legal theories drive these suiciderelated suits: state negligence law and federal due process law. Although no reported appellate decision in the state courts of North Carolina or in the federal Fourth Circuit Court of Appeals has as yet imposed liability on a school system for the self-inflicted death of a student under either of these theories, there is no reason to expect that this area will remain dormant.

Educators claim, and "history shows that, no matter what a school official chooses to do, someone will be unhappy."This may be due, in part, to the wide scope of duties that school officials are charged to carry out. School officials must, among other things, adequately supervise both students and employees, properly investigate and train prospective employees, and provide emergency medical care for injuries occurring on school grounds.

Though not legally obligated to guarantee the safety of their students, school officials are required to provide a degree of protection and attention to all students. In practical terms, this means that their actions (or their failure to act), as well as school board policies, will be closely scrutinized following a student's suicide. The lengths to which a school system must go to ensure the safety of its students will depend upon the jurisdiction's precedent (i.e., stare decisis)and statutes.

Several state courts evaluate these situations on a case by case basis.At least one state court has flatly refused to hold its school systems liable for negligence in any student suicide, regardless of the facts of the case.Following is a detailed discussion of both of the relevant theories of liability, negligence, and due process, and the reception of each in various jurisdictions in cases involving student suicide.

Negligence

Negligence is defined as "the failure to use such care as a reasonably prudent and careful person would use under similar circumstances."It consists of either "the doing of some act which a person of ordinary prudence would not have done under similar circumstances or failure to do what a person of ordinary prudence would have done under similar circumstances."

Negligence Cause of Action

For a negligence cause of action to be successful, a plaintiff must prove each of the following elements: (1) that a duty of care was owed by the defendant to the plaintiff; (2) that this duty of care was breached by the defendant; (3) that there was a causal connection between this breach and the plaintiff's injury; and (4) that an actual loss, damage, or injury to the plaintiff resulted from the defendant's breach of duty.

Although the elements of duty and breach are closely interwoven in the evaluation of a plaintiff's claim-without a duty there can be no breach; without a breach there can be no legal harm to be redressed-the two are in fact distinct. If no duty exists, the behavior of the defendant, even if apparently egregious, will never be at issue. The case will end before reaching trial. If a duty is found to exist, however, the behavior of the defendant, even if apparently benign, must be examined for a breach of duty. The case likely will go to trial.

Duty

A legal duty is an "obligation to conform to legal standards of reasonable conduct in light of apparent risk."This standard of reasonable conduct is often referred to as a standard of care. North Carolina teachers are "held to the same standard of care which a person of ordinary prudence, charged with the teacher's duties, would exercise in the same circumstances."The level of care required to satisfy that standard varies, however, according to the particular facts and circumstances of each case. For example, teachers have a duty to adequately supervise their pupils, and thus the school board that employs them can be held liable for "foreseeable injuries that result from a lack of teacher supervision."

A reasonably prudent teacher would keep a more careful eye on a young child than on an older child. Similarly, a distraught child would receive more supervision than would a student who appeared to be calm and contented. Teachers are not required "to anticipate the myriad of unexpected acts which occur daily in and about schools and school premises."In every case based on negligence, courts and juries must determine the standard of reasonable care demanded in a particular situation. Factors that weigh in this decision include the "foreseeability of an injury, the hazardousness of the activity, expert opinions in the field about what is reasonable under the circumstances, and the pertinent statutory or regulatory standards of care."

Foreseeability and the standard of care. North Carolina law focuses upon whether the injury-whether a student's broken leg or a suicide-was reasonably foreseeable. The common law classified suicide, or self-murder, as a felony along with conventional murder. Thus courts faced with "suicide claims allegedly resulting from a defendant's negligent act" consistently held that the defendant's civil liability ended with the act of suicide. Because suicide was considered a criminal act, courts reasoned that it "was typically not the foreseeable result of any alleged negligence."Even now, after the decriminalization of suicide, courts remain "rather reluctant to recognize suicide as a proximate consequence of a defendant's wrongful act." Suicide is often still "viewed as 'an independent, intervening act which the original tortfeasor could not have reasonably [been] expected to foresee.' "

A Case Study of a Negligence Cause of Action

Perhaps the first case in which a school district was found liable for negligence in a student's suicide was decided in 1995.Wyke v. Polk County School Board concerned a thirteen-year-old student, Shawn Wyke, who hanged himself in his backyard. A few days before, he had twice attempted to hang himself on school grounds, during school hours.

The appellate court, construing the evidence in light most favorable to the plaintiff, determined that school officials were made "somewhat aware" of both incidents but had "failed to hold Shawn in protective custody, failed to provide or procure counseling services for Shawn, and failed to notify [his family] of the attempts." Around the time of his suicide, Wyke's family was aware that he was angry and experiencing some emotional and behavioral problems. An appointment had been made for him to see a mental health counselor, but his family was unaware of his suicidal intent.

The district court dismissed the plaintiff's federal due process claims but sent the negligence and wrongful death claims to the jury. The jury found for the plaintiff, the district court entered judgment on the verdict, and the Eleventh Circuit Court of Appeals affirmed, holding that "both the evidence and the law" supported holding the school board liable for Wyke's death.

Under Florida law, like North Carolina law, school administrators have a duty to supervise students. The Wyke court found that this duty was violated when school administrators, with their degree of knowledge and authority, failed to act as reasonable people would have acted under similar circumstances. As to foreseeability, the court noted that if "ever there was a situation where a 'person of ordinary prudence' would recognize 'an acute emotional state, ' this was it."Although it is true that the "workings of the human mind are truly an enigma, " the court made it clear that neither it nor the jury believed "that a prudent person would have needed a crystal ball to see that Shawn needed help and that if he didn't get it soon, he might attempt suicide again."

The court held that Wyke's death was caused by this breach of duty (1) actually, because but for the administrators' failure to adequately supervise Wyke it is reasonable to assume that he would have received additional supervision and care from his family, and (2) proximately, because it was foreseeable to any reasonable person that Wyke might attempt suicide again and eventually might be successful. The damage from the administrator's breach was clear: Wyke's death.

Defenses to a Negligence Cause of Action

Contributory Negligence

Verdicts splitting liability between plaintiffs and defendants, of which the Wyke case is an example, are currently impossible in North Carolina. Wyke was decided under the laws of Florida, one of forty-six states operating under systems of comparative negligence, which "compare the fault attributable to the plaintiff to the fault attributable to the defendant and provide for the division of damages."

North Carolina operates under a contributory negligence system. This system does not allow negligent plaintiffs to succeed in actions against negligent defendants, regardless of the proportions of fault. A plaintiff who contributes to her injuries will not recover damages, even if her fault was comparatively small in relation to the fault of the defendant. In practical terms, this means that even if a defendant school board was ninety-five percent responsible for a student's death and his parents were 5 percent responsible, the parents would be unable to recover anything from the school board.

Governmental Immunity

Even if a school board would otherwise be found liable

for a student's suicide, it may, in proper circumstances, assert governmental immunity and escape liability. The government and its agents are immune from suit except to the extent that the government consents to liability. Because a board of education is a governmental agency, it is not liable in a tort or negligence action unless it has waived its governmental immunity pursuant to statutory authority.

In North Carolina, governmental immunity is addressed in Section 115C-42 of the North Carolina General Statutes:

> Any local board of education by securing liability insurance . . . is hereby authorized . . . to waive its governmental immunity from liability for damage by reason of death or injury to person or property caused by the negligence or tort of any agent or employee of such board of education. . . . [Governmental] immunity shall be deemed to have been waived by the act of obtaining such insurance, but such immunity is waived only to the extent that said board of education is indemnified by insurance for such negligence or tort.

The North Carolina Court of Appeals has ruled that the "primary purpose" of this statute was "to encourage local school boards to waive immunity by obtaining insurance protection while, at the same time, giving such boards the discretion to determine whether and to what extent to waive immunity."

Liability Based on Due Process

The Fourteenth Amendment to the United States Constitution provides that "no State shall . . . deprive any person of life, liberty, or property without due process of law . . . " This Due Process Clause offers constitutional safeguards to persons affected by governmental actions or judgments.

Both procedural and substantive due process must be satisfied for a government action affecting life, liberty, or property to be constitutional. Procedural due process stipulates how government actions are to be carried out. It requires that specific safeguards be fulfilled before a government action affecting life, liberty, or property can take place.Substantive due process, by contrast, is a generalized protection requiring governmental actions affecting life, liberty, or property to be "fair and reasonable in content as well as application." When a governmental action is both unfair or unreasonable and damaging to life, liberty, or property, it is said to violate substantive due process.

In student suicide cases, claims typically center on the school system's failure to take steps that would have prevented the suicide. A major hurdle for these plaintiffs is that substantive due process does not require the government to guarantee any one person's safety. The Due Process Clause "generally confers no affirmative right to governmental aid, even where such aid may be necessary to secure life, liberty, or property interests of which the government itself may not deprive the individual."

Plaintiffs may overcome this hurdle, however, by invoking an affirmative right to government protection under the Due Process Clause. Courts have recognized such an affirmative right where a "special relationship" exists between a state and the individual or where a "state-created danger" exists.

Section 1983: The Enforcement Mechanism

The Fourteenth Amendment does not, in itself, guarantee that due process violations will be actionable in a court of law. For the enforcement of these and other constitutionally granted rights, another mechanism is necessary. This mechanism, Section 1983 of Chapter 42 of the United States Code, provides that:

> Every person who, under the color of any statute, ordinance, regulation, custom, or usage, of any State . . . subjects, or causes to be subjected, any citizen of the United States or other person within the jurisdiction thereof to the deprivation of any rights, privileges, or immunities secured by the Constitution and laws, shall be liable to the party injured in an action at law, suit in equity, or other proper proceeding for redress . . . .

This short paragraph, commonly known as Section 1983, creates no new cause of action; no new rights were born with its passage.It is a neutral device which "merely provides 'a method for vindicating federal rights elsewhere conferred.'"Nevertheless, it has had an enormous impact on the federal court system; it has been said that a complete catalog of "constitutional claims that have been alleged under § 1983 would encompass numerous and diverse topics and subtopics."

Among these topics are the "mistreatment of school-children, deliberate indifference to the medical needs of prison inmates, the seizure of chattels without advance notice or sufficient opportunity to be heard-to identify only a few."Though deemed necessary for "deterring unconstitutional uses of state power, "Section 1983 cases have sometimes overwhelmed federal dockets.

Analysis of Section 1983 in the Context of School Board Liability for Student Suicides

Courts have held school employees, including teachers and school board members, to be proper "persons" subject to suit under Section 1983.According to the Supreme Court, acting under "color of state law" traditionally requires that a defendant "exercised power 'possessed by virtue of state law and made possible only because the wrongdoer is clothed with the authority of state law.' " This element excludes "merely private conduct, no matter how discriminatory or wrongful"from the reach of a Section 1983 cause of action.

The clause "shall be liable to the party injured" is what permits constitutional pronouncements like the Fourteenth Amendment to be enforced in federal courts.

Section 1983 and Student Suicide Actions

Plaintiffs in student suicide cases wishing to pursue substantive due process claims may reach federal courts through Section 1983. A federal Section 1983 claim may be attractive to plaintiffs for many reasons; including the following:

(a) It offers the option of conducting the suit in a federal court. If the pertinent state court is unsympathetic to liability cases involving student suicide, a plaintiff may seek redress in a federal forum.

(b) Some statespecific immunities and defenses are not pertinent to a Section 1983 claim. For example, as previously noted, a North Carolina plaintiff suing under a state negligence claim will recover nothing if found to be even 1 percent contributorally negligent. Contributory negligence is not applicable, however, in a Section 1983 claim arising from the same incident. State-based governmental immunity also is irrelevant in a Section 1983 suit. Federal law alone determines immunity in regard to Section 1983 claims. This is because allowing states to immunize violations of federal law would "transmute a basic guarantee into an illusory promise."

(c) The prevailing plaintiff in a Section 1983 cause of action is permitted to recover reasonable attorney fees. This is contrary to the traditional American rule, which holds that each party, win or lose, will be responsible for their own legal fees. State negligence claims operate under the American rule.

Despite the aforementioned advantages to filing suit under a Section 1983, this avenue is not a magical road to recovery. While it is common for violations of constitutional rights to be labeled as "constitutional torts, "the Due Process Clause "does not transform every tort committed by a state actor into a constitutional violation."Additional requirements beyond the ordinary tort elements must be met for a Section 1983 cause of action to be successful. Also, plaintiffs may be sabotaged by the same difficulties that haunt ordinary negligence suits. Two recent cases will help demonstrate the complexities of a Section 1983 cause of action.

The case of Armijo v. Wagon Mound Public Schools involved a sixteen-year-old special education student, Philadelfio Armijo, who was suspended for threatening a teacher.The school's principal, Mary Schutz, notified police of the suspension and asked them to detain Armijo if he was caught returning to school. Contrary to stated school disciplinary policy, however, Schutz did not attempt to notify Armijo's parents of the suspension. Instead she told the school's counselor, Tom Herrera, to drive Armijo home immediately. Herrera knew that Armijo had access to firearms and observed that Armijo was very angry as he was being driven home. Still, Herrera made no attempt to contact Armijo's parents or to check to see if they were home before leaving Armijo. Armijo had made a practice of confiding in a school aide, Pam Clouthier. Several times that fall, and on the day of this suspension, Armijo told her that "maybe I'd be better off dead." Clouthier apparently did not inform any school official of these threats.

Armijo's parents returned home to find their son dead of a selfinflicted gunshot wound to the chest. They subsequently filed suit in federal court against Schutz, Herrera, Clouthier, and the school district claiming a violation of Armijo's substantive due process rights.While, in general, substantive due process does not mean that school officials must guarantee a student's safety, Armijo's parents pointed out that in two particular circumstances, both recognized by the U.S. Supreme Court in DeShaney v. Winnebago, such an affirmative duty may indeed fall to school officials. One such circumstance is where school officials have entered into a "special relationship" with the student; the other is where school officials have themselves created the danger.

The special relationship exception to the general rule that governments have no obligation to protect their citizens from danger was created by the following passage in the DeShaney opinion:

> When the State takes a person into its custody and holds him there against his will, the Constitution

> imposes upon it a corresponding duty to assume some responsibility for his safety and general well-being. . . .

It is the State's affirmative act of restraining the individual's freedom to act on his own behalf- through incarceration, institutionalization, or other similar restraint of personal liberty-which is the "deprivation of liberty" triggering the protections of the Due Process Clause, not its failure to act to protect his liberty interests against harms inflicted by other means.

Almost all courts have interpreted this language to mean that a "special relationship" can exist only in custodial situations.Armijo had been restricted from returning to school on the day of his death, but "[b]anning a student from the school grounds does not rise to the same level of involuntary restraint as arresting, incarcerating, or institutionalizing an individual."Even had Armijo been in the custody of Herrera while confined in his car during the drive home from school, Armijo's suicide occurred after he had been released from the car and "was no longer under any involuntary restraint by a school official."Therefore the Armijo court held that no special relationship existed between Armijo and the defendants at the time of his death.

The danger creation exception grew out of the Supreme Court's comment in DeShaney, that even though "the State may have been aware of the dangers that [the plaintiff, a child severely abused by his father] faced in the free world, it played no part in their creation, nor did it do anything to render him any more vulnerable to them."This comment has been interpreted-perhaps stretched-to mean that a state may be liable for an individual's injury "if it created the danger that harmed the individual."Merely creating the danger is not enough, however; "the danger creation theory must ultimately rest on the specifics of a substantive due process claim-i.e. a claim predicated on reckless or intentional injury causing state action which 'shocks the conscience.' "

When deciding if the facts of a particular case shock the conscience, a court must bear in mind certain principles highlighted by the Supreme Court. These are "(1) the need for restraint in defining [the] scope [of substantive due process claims]; [and] (2) the concern that § 1983 not replace state tort law."To constitute a substantive due process violation, therefore, an action must be more deliberate, damaging, and outrageous than an ordinary tort.

The Armijo court articulated a six-part test to determine whether a defendant had created a special danger for the plaintiff:

> Plaintiff must demonstrate that (1) [Plaintiff] was a member of a limited and specifically definable group; (2) Defendants' conduct put [Plaintiff] . . . at substantial risk of serious, immediate and proximate harm; (3) the risk was obvious or known; (4) Defendants acted recklessly in conscious disregard of that risk; and (5) such conduct when viewed in total is conscience shocking. Also, in light of DeShaney, (6) Plaintiff must demonstrate that "the charged state entity and the charged individual defendant actors created the danger or increased the plaintiff's vulnerability to the danger in some way."

The Armijo court held that, where Schutz and Herrera were concerned, the facts of the plaintiffs' case could be construed as conscience shocking under this test but that Clouthier could not be held liable under a danger creation theory.The court thus sent the claims against Schutz and Herrera back to the district court for trial.

The second case, Hasenfus v. LaJeunesse, concerned a cluster of attempted suicides at a middle school in Maine, where seven students attempted suicide in a three-month period. Several of the attempts occurred at school or at school events. The school responded by not responding; no special counseling or monitoring programs were set up within the school, and no special information was provided to parents about the rash of incidents.

At the end of the three-month period, another incident occurred. Jamie Hasenfus tried to hang herself in the school locker room after being sent there alone for misconduct during a physical education class. The fourteen-year-old survived but was left with permanent impairments. Hasenfus had been raped at the age of thirteen and had testified against the rapist. School officials were aware of the rape and that she was an acquaintance of at least two of the students who previously had attempted suicide. Hasenfus's parents brought suit against the town, its board of education, the superintendent of schools, the school principal, and the gym teacher who sent her into the locker room alone. Their 1983 cause of action charged that "specific acts and omissions by defendants acting under color of state law deprived Jamie of her Fourteenth Amendment rights, including, [among other things], rights to life and physical safety."The parents also claimed that their own right to family integrity had been violated.A federal magistrate judge and the district court ruled that even if all these facts were true, the plaintiffs could not recover damages under Section 1983. The district court therefore dismissed the Section 1983 claims.

On appeal the First Circuit agreed with the lower court and affirmed its judgment. DeShaney unequivocally stated that "[t]he affirmative duty to protect arises not from the State's knowledge of the individual's predicament or from its expressions of intent to help him, but from the limitation which it has imposed on his freedom to act on his own behalf."Therefore, the courts found that the school's knowledge of Hasenfus's depression and the alarming rash of suicide attempts were not enough to create a special relationship. The Hasenfus court emphasized that the special relationship rule is unique, usually applying to persons who, like incarcerated prisoners or involuntarily committed mental patients, are obviously in the custody of the state.

Almost every court that has considered the issue has refused to base a custodial relationship on compulsory attendance laws.Although the Hasenfus court rejected the attempt by these particular plaintiffs to liken a student's situation to that of a prisoner or patient, it did leave open the possibility of creating a mandatory attendance/ custodial special relationship. In a highly unusual passage, the court stated that it was "loath to conclude now and forever that inaction by a school toward a pupil could never give rise to a due process violation, " noting that "[f]or limited purposes and for a portion of the day, students are entrusted by their parents to the control and supervision of teachers in situations where-at least as to very young children- they are manifestly unable to look after themselves." If a young child fell down an elevator shaft, the court wondered, "could the school principal ignore the matter?"This reasoning invokes, perhaps deliberately, the "deliberate indifference" theory already used to establish municipal liability under Section 1983.

The deliberate indifference theory holds a defendant responsible only for injuries that the defendant knew were likely and could have prevented or reduced. Inaction incurs liability "only where the recipient's response to the [situation] or lack thereof is clearly unreasonable in light of the known circumstances;"this is very near to the "shock the conscience" standard already entrenched in examining a special relationship.

Suicide among Adults

Few things are more disturbing than the death of a child. Even more upsetting is the death of a child by his or her own hand. An unfortunate characteristic of American culture since 1950 has been the increasing number of its population that completes suicide. For example, in 1990, 30, 906 people completed suicide in the United States. In addition, steady increases in completed suicides have been documented over the past 4 decades in virtually every age group (0 -14, 15 -24, 25 -40, 41 -55, 56 -70, and more than 70) studied. While the 15 -24-year-olds (adolescents and young adults) ranked third in 1994 among all age groups in the total number of suicides (4, 869), they ranked second lowest in rate of suicide (a calculation per 100, 000 people) among all age groups.

The incidence of suicide has grown dramatically since 1955 and is now considered the second leading cause of death among adolescents and young adults. In addition, historical patterns appear in the study of suicide among the 15-to 24-year-old age group. Higher rates of suicide were observed in the 1930s (the Great Depression), lower rates in the 1940s (World War II), and steady growth rates from the 1950s to the present. Cross-cultural data concerning the incidence of suicide shows a drastic increase from the ages of 5 -14 to 15 -24.

Table 1

Significant Risk Factors Associated With Adolescent Suicide

1.	Psychiatric disorders such as depression and anxiety.
2.	Drug and alcohol abuse.
3.	Genetic factors.
4.	Family loss or disruption.
5.	Friend or family member of suicide victim.
6.	Homosexuality.
7.	Rapid sociocultural change.
8.	Media emphasis on suicide.
9.	Impulsiveness and aggressiveness.
10.	Ready access to lethal methods.

In addition, gender effects appear cross-culturally, for males have a higher rate of completed suicide at nearly every age level.

Hidden within the overall group of adolescents are subgroups with a higher rate of suicide than the average rate for the entire group. For example, the most startling estimates of subgroups of adolescents were forwarded by Alessi, McManus, Brickman, and Grapentine, who found that 61% of juvenile defenders attempted suicide, and Tomlinson-Keasey and Keasey, who estimated that 33% of troubled adolescents in their study attempted suicide. From these and other studies we can conclude that the rate of adolescent suicide has risen over the past 4 decades, as have the rates of other groups. We can also conclude that subgroups within the adolescent and young adult group vary in their rate of suicide.

The field of suicidology has made considerable strides in determining the rates of suicide among differing groups of people, researching the salient events and circumstances surrounding suicide, as well as the cataloging of characteristics shared by the victims of suicide. As evidence to this claim, Hollinger and Offer noted that the literature base on suicide doubled from 1969 to 1980.

Epidemiological research suggests that males have a higher rate of completed suicide at nearly every age level. Individuals are considered at-risk for suicide when they present a variety of risk factors and begin thinking about or planning on taking their own lives. Salient risk factors related to suicide include psychiatric disorders; family relations; family history of psychiatric disorders, suicide, or both; abuse of drugs, alcohol, or both; environmental stresses; exposure to other attempts; social isolation; homosexuality; prior suicidal behaviour; and firearms present within the home.

Schuckit and Schuckit examined substance use and abuse as a risk factor in adolescent suicide. Controlled substances, alcohol, or both are frequently used as the means of self-harm or as a prelude to a suicidal act, contributing to reduced inhibitions, increased impulsivity, and impaired judgment. Socioeconomic factors associated with high risk of suicide include exposure to high levels of stress, especially at an early age. Such stresses include loss of social supports through death, parental separation or divorce, change in school environments, and problems with peer relationships.

Holinger et al. reviewed retrospective and prospective research on suicide and found that most individuals who kill themselves meet criteria for diagnosable psychiatric disorders, including affective disorders (25 -75%), personality disorders (25 -40%), or both. The diagnoses in these cases were, however, ade after the suicide. In fact, one study reported that "only 24%of completed suicides (male and female, all ages) had been in contact with ental health services within the past two years". The comorbidity of affective disorders, personality disorders, substance abuse, or some combination of these two factors appears to be particularly lethal.

Approximately 25 -50%of adolescents completing suicide have a family history of psychiatric disorders, suicides, or both, and 25 -50% have previously attempted to take their own lives. The number and lethality of attempts were also found to correlate positively with completed suicide. In addition, when firearms were found within the home, a marked increase in the risk of suicide was observed. Sexual identity issues, such as homosexuality, also increased the risk of suicide among adolescents. Research has indicated that suicide completers tend to be brighter than average.

A variety of psychologists proposed alternative theories about why adolescence is a time of contemplation of suicide for some. First and foremost, suicide has been linked to the presence of depression. For individuals who are depressed, suicide may be seen as a viable option. For example, Golombek studied the relationship of depression, risk of suicide, and personality in what he identified as three stages of adolescence. According to Sargent, Golombek theorized that

> Depression is expressed differently in each of three stages of adolescence. In early adolescence, depression may be manifested by anger and disorganized or erratic behaviour. In mid-adolescence, a stage of rebellion, depression may be seen in exaggerated autonomy and angry outbursts. Later adolescence brings a "new sense of separateness, "with disillusionment, dissatisfaction, and a sense of loss. During this period, depression is

more typically expressed by feelings of sadness and guilt and is more self-directed.

Therefore, Golombek viewed late adolescence as the time that suicide could most likely result from depression, thereby explaining the increased incidence of suicide at this stage of development. Shneidman discussed four elements of suicide:

(a) heightened inimicality,

(b) exacerbation of perturbation,

(c) increased constriction of intellectual focus (tunnelling or narrowing of the mind's content) , and

(d) cessation.

Inimicality involves "qualities within the individual that are unfriendly toward the self ", or ways in which the individual is his or her own enemy, such as engaging in self-destructive behaviours. According to Shneidman, perturbation refers to "how disturbed, 'shook up, 'ill at ease, or mentally upset a person is". Dichotomous thinking, blocking out memories of the past, or avoiding thought about how others would be affected are examples of constriction. Shneidman identified the concept of cessation as the spark that ignites the above potentially explosive mixture. Cessation involves the idea that one can put a stop to his or her pain, thereby producing a perceived solution for the desperate individual.

Psychodynamic explanations, such as Freud's, have viewed suicide as internal conflict of aggression turned upon one's self. A suicide attempt ay also be the expression of aggression against an internalized object. A more contemporary psychodynamic theory of suicide is that adolescents who complete suicide escape conflict and stress. Evidence of the influence stress can have on the incidence of suicide includes the historical patterns apparent in the field of suicidology. For example, higher rates of suicide were observed during the Great Depression, a time of great stress.

Humanistic theories purport that, "provided basic needs are met, humans are essentially growth-oriented creatures whose nature is directed toward realizing their potential if external conditions permit ". Therefore, suicidal adolescents may have difficulty fulfilling their basic needs. Existential theory focuses on the difficulty individuals can have in finding meaning in their lives. Inability to discover meaning in life can also lead to feelings of uselessness, hopelessness, and depression. These feelings can, in turn, lead to suicide .

One cognitive explanation for suicide suggests that, when adolescents lack adequate problem-solving skills and face stress-provoking problems, they develop an attitude of hopelessness and eventually attempt suicide because they see no other alternative. Holmes described this process as follows: An inability to solve their problems can lead adolescents to feelings of hopelessness, which can be closely related to suicide. Once cognitively rigid adolescents decide on suicide as a solution to their problems, they will pursue only that solution and not consider or develop alternative solutions.

Stillion and McDowell integrated many of the above theories in their Suicide Trajectory Model, which includes four main categories of risk factors that should be examined when working with suicidal adolescents: biological (e. g., depression, genetic factors, male gender) , psychological (e. g., depression, low self-esteem, hopelessness, existential issues, poor coping strategies), cognitive (e. g., developmental level, negative self-talk, cognitive rigidity, generalization, selective abstraction, inexact labelling), and environmental (e. g. , negative family experiences, negative life events, loss, presence of firearms). Along with influencing the occurrence of suicide among adolescents, these risk factors may also influence each other. For example, an adolescent who has encountered negative family experiences may, in turn, have poor coping strategies. Stillion and McDowell described the influence of the factors identified in their model of suicidal ideation, gestures, and attempts in adolescents.

> As we love through life, we encounter situations and events that add their weight to each risk factor category. When the combined weight of these risk factors reaches the point where coping skills are threatened with collapse, suicidal ideation is born. Once present, suicidal ideation seems to feed upon itself. It may be exhibited in warning signs and may be intensified by trigger events. In the final analysis, however, when the suicide attempt is made, it occurs because of the contributions of the four risk categories.

Suicide of Gifted Adolescents and Young Adults

Table 2 includes six reasons that there have been few studies conducted on the suicides of gifted students. Dixon and Scheckel summarized current thinking about the characteristics of gifted adolescents often associated with risk of suicide. They include perfectionism, isolationism related to extreme introversion, unusual sensitivity and perfectionism, and the five over excitibilities (psychomotor, sensual, intellectual, imaginational, and emotional) identified by Dabrowski as part of his Theory of Positive Disintegration and elaborated on by Piechowski.

Table 2
Reasons Few Studies Have Been Conducted on the Suicides of Gifted Students

1.	The current data collected nationally about adolescent suicide does not include if the child was gifted.
2.	The varying definitions of gifted and talented used across the United States make it difficult to know if a child who completed suicide was gifted.
3.	Issues of confidentiality limit access to data.
4.	Conducting psychological autopsies of suicide victims is an expensive endeavour in terms of time and money.
5.	Conducting research on this topic is more difficult because more adolescent-aged students than preadolescents complete suicide, combined with the fact that secondary schools, colleges, and universities are not as actively engaged in identifying gifted students.
6.	The terminal nature of suicide requires certain types of information to be garnered after the event.

Suicide and gifted students through the lens of humanistic psychology. Hayes and Sloat investigated the prevalence of suicide among gifted students across 69 schools in a four-county region. They found that 8 of the 42 cases of attempted suicide were among gifted students, but none actually died by suicide. Parker and Adkins found that students in honours colleges demonstrated significantly higher scores on subscales of an instrument measuring neurotic perfectionism. They questioned whether elevated perfectionism is indicative of a "predisposition to maladjustment or is a healthy component of the pursuit of academic excellence among the highly able ".

Two studies drew on longitudinal data from the Terman sample focusing on the suicides of females.

Discriminant function analyses were performed in both studies, yielding "signatures of suicide. "The signatures included in the analysis -previous suicide attempts, anxiety, depression, temperament, ental health, loss of a father before age 20, stress in the family of origin, physical health, and alcohol abuse -correctly classified 37 of 40 participants. These signatures inform the knowledge base about gifted adult females of a certain generation who were determined to be gifted using Terman's notion of giftedness from the 1920s.

According to Cross, the following can be said about the suicide of gifted adolescents.

1. Adolescents are committing suicide; therefore, gifted adolescents are committing suicide.

2. The rate of suicide has increased over the past decades for the general population of adolescents within the context of an overall increase across all age groups; therefore, it is reasonable to conclude that the incidence of suicide among gifted adolescents has increased over the past decade, keeping in mind that there are no definitive data available on the subject.

3. Given the limited data available, we cannot ascertain whether the incidence of suicide among gifted adolescents is different than in the general population of adolescents.

While establishing incidence rates of suicide and describing the factors associated with suicide among gifted adolescents are important, another important goal of suicidology is to describe the lives 'of suicide victims. To that end, a variety of case studies of gifted students have been carried out in an attempt to shed light on the suicidal behaviour of the subjects. One of the most promising approaches to studying the lives of gifted adolescents who have completed suicide is the psychological autopsy.

For most teens in modem American society adolescence is a difficult time, full of change and challenge. Changes in school, changes in relationships with peers, renegotiations of their roles in the family, and the physical changes that accompany puberty all come crashing in together. Perhaps most important, a crucial developmental task of adolescence is the formation of a personal identity-a sense of self, a personal value system, and an independent place in society.

Teens with resilience and good coping skills usually sail through these stormy seas with minimal difficulty, but an alarming proportion of teens respond to the stress of this period by attempting suicide. According to the latest data, suicide is the eighth leading cause of death among Americans of all ages but is the third leading cause of death among, 15- to 24-year-olds and the second leading cause of death among white males in this age group.

In 1998 4,003 youth aged 15 to 24 years took their own lives, and experts estimate that perhaps as many as 200 times that number made unsuccessful suicide attempts. Six to 13% of teens report that they have attempted suicide at least once. Even more alarming is the fact that the incidence of suicide among adolescents and young adults nearly tripled from 1952 to 1995, while the overall suicide rate in the U. S. increased less than 20%.

One of the primary tasks for teens in their quest for personal identity is their search for sexual identity. In a recent study more than one quarter of 12-year-olds, felt uncertain about their sexual orientation (vs. 5% of 18 year olds). In contrast to this uncertainty, most gay, lesbian and bisexual (GLB) individuals are first aware of sexual orientation by age 10, with self labelling of sexual orientation around ages 14 to 15.

Although most GLB teens also learn to cope with the pressures of identity development and become healthy adults, published surveys report that 20% to 66% of homosexual respondents attempt suicide at least once, with a mean of about one third. Gay teens account for 30 to 50% of all completed suicide attempts among American youth-approximately one every six hours.

Until recently, the question of whether GLB teens are at increased risk of suicide has been a matter of debate. Although at least 10 peer-reviewed studies have found high rates of suicide attempts among GLB teens (from 20 to 67%), the generalizability of these studies has been questioned because of potential bias in the convenience samples employed, dependence on retrospective designs, etc. More recent studies, however, have employed population-based sampling (many as part of the CDC Youth Risk Behaviour Survey in several states). GLB teens in these studies report attempting suicide 2 to 14 times more than heterosexuals, corroborating earlier findings. Two recent studies of large population-based cohorts suggest that the true lifetime risk of suicide attempts for homosexuals is approximately six times that of their peers.

GLB teens also make more lethal suicide attempts than their heterosexual peers. More than one in five GLB suicide attempts studied by Remafedi, Farrow and Deisher resulted in medical or psychiatric hospitalization, compared to the 1 to 2% rate reported in most studies of youth suicide attempts. GLB teens also have higher rates of reattempted suicide (20 to 52%).

What's it like to be a gay, lesbian or bisexual teenager in your school? For many it is a life of disapproval, rejection, isolation, discrimination and abuse. Surveys of community-based samples of GLB teens have shown that as many as 80% of the respondents have been verbally harassed, 43% have had an object thrown at them, 17% have been physically assaulted, and 10% have been assaulted with a weapon-all because of their sexual orientation. Almost half (40%) of one sample reported that verbal abuse occurred daily.

In a recent population-based survey in Massachusetts, students who reported engaging in same-sex behaviour were 3. 4 times as likely as their peers to have skipped school because they felt unsafe, 5. 5 times as likely to have been threatened or injured with a weapon 4 or more times at school, and 2. 9 times as likely to have been in a physical fight at school. Some 28% of homosexual youth drop out of secondary school because of discomfort and fear. As much as half of GLB respondents in other studies report they have heard teachers or other school staff make homophobic remarks. Homosexual teens are not even safe at home -- 40% of the Pilkington and D'Augelli respondents reported verbal abuse from family members, and 10% reported physical assaults from family members. Kevin Jennings, executive director of the Gay, Lesbian & Straight Education Network, has called this "an epidemic of harassment and violence".

Negative attitudes toward homosexuals and even discrimination are, of course, widespread in American society. A 1998 Gallup poll revealed that the majority of Americans (59%) believe that homosexuality is morally wrong. Fully 89% of the 15 to 19-year-old respondents in a 1988 national survey agreed that sex between two men was "disgusting, " and only 12% felt confident that they could befriend a gay person. The recent case of Matthew Shepherd, a gay youth who was tied to a fence, pistol whipped, and left to die by two other young men, comes immediately to mind. Taken collectively, these data paint a stark picture of the life of many GLB teenagers. In such a world it is easy to understand why GLB teens often respond with depression, anxiety, substance abuse, and lack of self-esteem, all of which can contribute to the decision to attempt suicide.

Many, perhaps most, GLB teens attempt to hide their sexual orientation because they see how gays are treated. These teens often pay an even higher emotional price than do openly gay teens, however, because leading a double life requires an immense emotional energy. Closeted teens also live with the constant fear of being discovered or being "outed" by those who know their secret. In addition, these teens are often out to some family members and not others, and this secret contributes to damaging already precarious family relationships.

One of the most common questions about homosexuality heard today is whether sexual orientation is determined by genetics or by early upbringing and societal influences (nature vs. nurture). For example, male homosexuality is widely believed to be the result of having a "strong" mother and a "weak" father.

Recent scientific studies, however, have convincingly demonstrated that homosexual orientation is not caused by adverse conditions in upbringing, such as abnormal parenting, sexual abuse, etc.. Recent polls show that Americans continue to lean toward the "nurture" rather than the "nature" explanation for sexual orientation by a 47 to 31% margin. In a Newsweek poll a similar proportion of Americans (33%) believed that homosexuality is "something people are born with, not the result of upbringing or environmental influences. " The proportion of Americans accepting a genetic explanation (only 13% in 1977), however, has increased substantially over time. In contrast, fully 75% of the gay respondents in the recent Newsweek poll endorsed the "nature" position.

Several recent studies have suggested that a substantial portion of sexual orientation can be accounted for by heredity. LeVay's discovery of physical differences in the autopsied brains of homosexual males compared to heterosexual males, for example, has received considerable attention even though all of the gay males in this study died of AIDS, which could have caused the observed dimorphism.

Twin studies have long been a preferred tool of geneticists for determining the heritability of a characteristic. If a trait is determined genetically, then identical (monozygotic-MZ) twins would be expected to share the trait (be concordant), while concordance between fraternal (dizygotic-DZ) twins would be expected to be less, approximating that of unrelated individuals such as adopted siblings. Combining the results of seven recent twin studies reveals that 141 of 244 MZ pairs (58%) in which at least one of the twins was homosexual were concordant for sexual orientation compared to 32 of 175 DZ pairs (18%). The concordance among adopted brothers of homosexuals included in one study was 11%. The few available reports of MZ twins raised apart suggest that the concordance for homosexuality is similar to that for MZ twins raised together. The preponderance of identical twins who are both homosexual, compared to the lower frequency of concordant fraternal twins which is more similar to adopted siblings, strongly supports the conclusion that homosexuality has a large heritable component. Based on these data, Pillard and Bailey calculate the heritability of sexual orientation as ranging between. 31 and. 74 (out of 1. 0).

The strongest evidence supporting genetic determination of homosexual orientation comes from the work of Hamer who performed molecular genetic studies on the chromosomes of 40 pairs of gay brothers. Among these siblings, a statistically significant number -- 33 pairs- had received the same region of their X chromosome (q28) from their mother (only 20 would have been expected by chance). Thus, not only had Hamer found evidence supporting the genetic heritability of homosexual orientation among these men, but he had mapped the determining locus (sometimes called the "gay gene") on the X chromosome, explaining earlier observations that homosexuality tends to occur in an X-linked pattern in some families. This research has been widely criticized on a number of counts, especially the selection of sibling pairs in which an X-linked pattern of inheritance of homosexuality was apparent a priori. Regardless of these criticisms, Hamer's work is now widely recognized as supporting the conclusion that, at least in some families, homosexual orientation has a strongly inherited component.

There is also ample evidence that non-genetic factors play an important role in determining sexual orientation in many cases. For example, although 11% concordance for homosexuality among adopted brothers in the Bailey and Pillard twin study mentioned above was somewhat less than the 18% concordance rate of DZ twins obtained by combining all studies to date, the adopted brother rate is at least double (and maybe triple) the incidence of homosexuality in the population at large, depending on the estimate used (Anonymous, undated). Given that DZ twins are genetically no more likely to be homosexual than are any two siblings, this difference is assumed to be environmental in origin. There is also evidence to suggest that a man's likelihood of being gay is directly proportional to the number of older brothers in his family (a non-genetic factor), which could be related to differential prenatal hormone exposure.

Biopsychosocial Model of Sexual Orientation Determination

Based on the weight of the evidence to date, modem behavioral geneticists generally favour a biopsychosocial model of sexual orientation: that it is determined by a combination of both genetic and environmental factors. Furthermore, genetic influences may be more important in some families than in others. This view is consistent with modem genetics which has shown that, in contrast to the simplified understanding of Mendelian inheritance in garden peas and fruit flies that we teach to most high school biology students, the majority of human traits are polygenic (determined in concert by several different genes) and multifactorial (influenced by many genetic and nongenetic factors).

A central dictum in this understanding is that a person's DNA (genetics) determines the capacity to express a trait; the environment determines the extent to which that trait is expressed. This modem view of heredity is not, however, widely endorsed, at least in the U. S. Only 6% of the respondents to the 1998 Gallup poll, for example, endorsed the position that both nature and nurture determine sexual orientation. On the other hand, when asked if homosexuality is "always due to the way a person is born, " "always due to factors such as upbringing or environment, " or if it "depends on the person, " fully 63% endorsed the third option, which is more consistent with the modern scientific view, with less than 20% choosing either the nature-only or nurture-only options.

Currently, there is a number of religious organizations that aim to help gays "go straight, " but evaluations of such programs have not been published, and their success rates are hotly debated. Perhaps the more important point to be made is, whether gays can change or not, the vast majority of homosexuals do not believe such change is possible.

Is Homosexuality Right or Wrong?

Both the natural and the social sciences can have much to say about homosexuality. Heterosexual behaviour is certainly the most common form of sexual expression (the "norm") in American society. On the other hand, homosexual behaviour has been reported in all human civilizations studied. As for the natural sciences, one of the most common arguments against homosexuality is the mistaken notion that same-sex behaviour does not occur among animals, i. e. that homosexuality is "unnatural" and therefore unacceptable/ immoral. A recent review of published field studies of mammals and birds, however, reveals that same-sex behaviour occurs in almost every species studied.

In fact, "exclusive homosexuality of various types occurs in more than 60 species of nondomesticated mammals and birds, including at least 10 kinds of primates and more than 20 other species of mammals". Sharing these facts with those who oppose positive attitudes toward homosexuals may, of course, have little effect because this knowledge can also be used to argue that homosexuality is a base or "animal" characteristic. As Weinrich has noted, "When animals do something that we like, we call it natural. When they do something that we don't like, we call it animalistic. "

Even if there were clear evidence that homosexuality is mostly determined genetically, the moral issue would not be settled. Those with pro-gay attitudes would likely conclude that being "born homosexual" is like being born left-handed and should be left alone. Those with anti-gay attitudes would conclude that being born gay is like being born with a congenital deformity-born "sick" and in need of treatment. These arguments make it clear that whether homosexuality is moral or immoral, normal or abnormal is a question that cannot be answered by science. The answer to the question is "entirely in the eye of the beholder".

How Can We Help?

All adolescents wonder about sexuality. They have concerns about their bodies and sexual feelings, and they wonder about what others do and think. Questions about sexual orientation are common. How can we help?

Start with a Personal Inventory

Self-understanding and self-awareness are the first step. How do you really feel about teen suicide, sexual orientation, and gay/lesbian and bisexual teen issues? Is there more information you need? Students are astute, and our attitudes and beliefs are often transparent to them. How important is acceptance of diversity to the welfare and education of our youth? What responsibility do biology teachers have to this educational goal? What is your duty toward potentially suicidal students? What are your personal beliefs and attitudes about homosexuality? Do you accept GLB sexuality as being within the range of normal behaviours, or do you believe that gays can and should change their sexual orientation? What are your moral and/or religious beliefs about homosexuality? Are your behaviours congruent with your beliefs and your ideological commitments to the welfare of students? In light of this self-reevaluation and what you have just read, are there beliefs or actions that you might want to change?

Responding uncritically and with unconditional positive regard toward students provides an atmosphere of respect and open exchange. Modelling honest acceptance of questions and respectful responses creates a safe arena for students to reflect on important personal questions that otherwise would not be asked. What kind of personal interactions do you have with students (combative, superior, accepting, concerned)? Do teens find you to be respectful of their concerns and questions?

More broadly, a teacher's choice of words is a crucial component of establishing a safe environment for all teenagers. We live in a culture that assumes that everyone is heterosexual. As products of that culture, teachers may unconsciously use terms that marginalize and exclude teens with same-sex attractions. It takes a concerted effort to use terms such as partner instead of girlfriend/boyfriend. Heterosexual students are not likely to notice the difference, but GLB teens certainly are.

Referring to heterosexuality, homosexuality and bisexuality as sexual orientations is also preferable to using the term sexual preference because the latter implies a personal belief that sexual orientation is chosen by the individual, as one might prefer rap music over heavy metal. Preferences lack stability and concreteness and are thus susceptible to change. Similarly, labelling homosexuality as a "lifestyle" implies to many that you accept a negative stereotypical view of all gay and lesbian individuals and implies a blanket disapproval. The lives of homosexuals are, of course, as varied as those of heterosexuals.

There are several ways to address sexual orientation explicitly in the biology classroom. The best, perhaps, is to discuss the current biological understandings of sexual orientation as an example of behavioral genetics. Be sure to include recent research including twin studies, same-sex behaviour across species, and the work of Hamer and others reviewed above. Be sure to acknowledge that most human heredity (including sexual orientation) is not determined by simple Mendelian alleles but is polygenic and multifactorial.

Sexual orientation, like evolution therefore, is an appropriate case example to use when teaching about the nature of science, the different kinds of questions asked by science and religion, the kinds of evidence required to answer scientific questions, etc. This is the place to be careful to point out that science takes no position on whether homosexual behaviour is right or wrong, although the scientific evidence about the causes of homosexuality and its occurrence can influence a person's opinions about such non-scientific questions. Making sure that your instruction focuses on the scientific questions and evidence and not on personal, moral or religious arguments is, of course, important and a solid basis for responding to any concerns that may be raised by parents or school officials.

AIDS is another common biological topic that often raises issues about homosexual behaviour. In the U. S. and other countries where the majority of HIV transmission has been among men who have sex with men, it is important to remind students that AIDS is a sexually transmitted disease, not an exclusively "gay disease. "

Heterosexual students who feel that AIDS only affects gay men can be lulled into a false sense of security when they believe they are unlikely targets of the AIDS virus. Some American students still carry a cultural hostility which holds that AIDS is an appropriate retribution for immoral behaviour or that gay men are to blame for the AIDS crisis. Here it might be good to review heterosexual statistics from around the world and to note that the HIV transmission rates among older (though not younger) American men who have sex with men have plummeted due to a widespread reduction of risk taking, while heterosexual transmission rates continue to rise.

GLB teens have very few positive role models. Here, too, the biology teacher can help by tangentially recognizing the sexual orientation of various homosexual scientists when their work is discussed, most especially when their sexual orientation relates directly to their work. Prominent homosexual scientists of the past include Leonardo da Vinci, Sir Francis Bacon and Alexander von Humbolt. In the 20th century, students may recognize Alan Turing (creator of the first modern computer), Margaret Mead (anthropologist and President of the AAAS), Bruce Voeller (biologist and AIDS researcher, pioneer of the use of nonoxynol-9 as a spermacide), and, of course, Dean Hamer.

Depending on your personal convictions, school policies, and administrators' positions, you might also consider recommending that a suicide prevention component be added to your school's health education curriculum. Encourage administrators to provide teachers with training on how to combat sexual harassment among students. Develop a list of local counselors, gay-supportive organizations, web sites and readings to share with GLB teens, and/or support a school gay/straight alliance. Most importantly, be available to talk with your students privately, maintain a supportive and accepting attitude, and honour their confidentiality.

The Internet has given teens a new, safe place to express their thoughts and feelings. It has helped them feel less alone by making connections with others in similar life situations. Many of them find it much easier to write and chat about their lives online than to talk to someone in person or even anonymously on the phone. For those who won't talk to anyone else, for whatever reasons, the Internet has proven to be a life-line.

The Internet has also provided unprecedented real-time access to their daily lives. They can chat and write about events in their homes as they are happening, or minutes after. Talking to them and listening to their stories years has helped to understand the cause and effect relationships between how they are treated and how they think, feel and act.

Abuse and Suicide

There is a direct and very strong connection between repeated abuse and suicidal feelings. In most cases there has been physical abuse up to around age 12. By then the fear of the parents is well established. After that, the abuse is primarily emotional. Sometimes, though, the physical and/or sexual abuse also continues up to the time the adolescent is legally able to leave the parents. By this point there is often almost nothing left of the person's self-worth and self-esteem. Even if they are still alive physically, their souls and spirits have been all but killed. It takes an exceptionally resilient person to survive 16 or 18 years of abuse, but some do. Others, however, find the emotional pain too great and either kill themselves or make repeated attempts to do so.

A major problem is that many of the abused teens are "only" being abused emotionally now, so social service workers do not put a high priority on such cases. They are simply too overworked. Another problem is that often they are not even aware of suicidal teens before it is too late. Even when they are aware they can do very little to fill the teens' unmet emotional needs or to stop their emotional pain. Psychiatrists often try to put the teen on medication. But medication does not fill their emotional needs, nor does it make their parents better fathers or mothers. As we say it, "Putting Megan on medication does not make Mom a better mother." This is so obvious, yet it needs to be said again and again until systems and beliefs are changed to reflect reality.

The greatest source of pain for these teens is feeling a lack of caring, respect, acceptance, support, and understanding from their own parents or gaurdians. To oversimplify, one can say it is coming from a lack of love - the love a parent normally gives those human beings entrusted to them. But the social services workers can't force parents/ guardians to give love. Nor can they force them to show caring, respect, acceptance, etc. Neither can they force them to feel caring, respectful, accepting towards their children and teens. If the feelings are not there, the behavior will never follow.

A social services worker in one country told that they never prosecute emotional abuse cases since they are so overworked with physical and sexual abuse cases. Emotional abuse is also harder to see than other forms of abuse, perhaps especially for those who have experienced it. Author Nicky Cruz, who was a gang leader in New York City, makes this point when he says that when was growing up he was "too young to realize that the wounds inflicted by withholding love penetrated far deeper even than irresponsible punishment..."

Emotional abuse is also harder to prove in a court of law. This seems to be a flaw in our child protection services. As mentioned, studies show that emotional abuse can be more damaging than physical abuse. Another problem is that society, in general, is not designed to give parents the emotional competency training which they need. Parents are not trained in emotional skills and they are not tested for emotional intelligence or emotional competency.

Fear for Reporting

The teens are highly resistant to reporting abuse in their homes. They have learned it is dangerous to tell the truth to anyone. They have learned not to trust adults. One of the most damaging forms of abuse is convincing a child or teen that it is dangerous to tell the truth. These young people have learned they will be attacked, invalidated, disbelieved and punished for telling the truth.

They have also been made to feel guilty for hurting their parents, breaking up families, etc. One 15 year old told that her fault for breaking up the family when she reported that her step-father was abusing her. She could have just put up with it till she was 16 when she could move out. It is difficult for anyone to admit that they have been abused. It is especially difficult when the abusers are your own parents. Teens know that they will be talked about; that everyone at school will find out. This is extremely hard on them. They all yearn to be "normal." They know they will be treated differently by their peers. They also know there will be investigations and lots of questions and it will be extremely uncomfortable at home. They are afraid of punishment and retaliation if they report their own parents.

For many teens, even if they thought the authorities would believe them, they know there is no place to go once they have told the truth about their own parents. This makes it much harder for the teen to report abuse .

Characteristics of Self-harming Teens

The following are some of the characteristics of depressed, suicidal and self-harming teens:

— They are intelligent. They question things. They want real answers. Too many times, though, they do not get answers which satisfy them.

— They are sensitive. They care about others They take on the pain from others.

— They are full of thoughts. They are full of fears. They feel trapped in their thoughts and fears.. They lay awake at night trying to figure things out.

— They are repeatedly invalidated. They have learned to lie about their feelings.

— They have no one with whom they can be totally honest, including emotionally honest.

— They are emotionally intense. Sometimes demanding and insistent. They are persistent. When their needs aren't met they later become "obsessive." Then they get judged, labeled, and criticized for this.

— They are afraid. Afraid of their parents, teachers, police, mental health professionals and peers.

— They see through false people. They see hypocrisy. They see injustice and are troubled .

— They feel controlled. They need more freedom than their peers but their parents give them less.

— They need more caring, understanding, emotional support and acceptance, but their parents give them less.

The purposes of developing the following procedures are to provide established guidelines and assistance to the teachers, parents, and others who can come in contact with students who may be at risk of committing suicide.

— Any student reporting he or she has suicidal thoughts should be referred to the Counseling Department or School Psychologist immediately. The faculty member who has become aware of this information must assume direct responsibility for reporting the information, just as in cases of suspected child abuse.

— Any District employee having any reason to believe a student is considering or threatening suicide must report this information to the Principal, School Psychologist, or Counseling Department immediately.

— Within one school day of receiving a report of potential suicide, a social worker, school psychologist or counselor must interview the student to:

a. Assess whether the student is in imminent danger, at moderate risk; or at low risk;

b. Provide support to the student; and

c. Inform the student that concern for the student's safety will be shared with his parents/guardians.

— After interviewing the student:

a. Report the interview to the Assistant Principal for Student Services and/or Dean of Students and to the Counseling Department Chair. The verbal report should be confirmed by a written memorandum.

b. Contact the parents/guardians for an interview

Following the intervention with the student and his or her family, the counselor or school psychologist will:

— Contact the principal and assistant principals and the health services coordinator to share pertinent details of the situation and determine whether the student's teachers should be informed

— Initiate follow-up contact with the parents/guardians to determine what actions were taken by the parents/guardians and obtain signed release of information forms to enable the social worker to contact the referral resources in order to coordinate services.

— Have a follow-up interview with the student to assess the student's condition and the parent's/guardian's response.

— Maintain regular contact with the student until the student is further evaluated by a mental health professional in the community and provide further assistance as recommended by the physician, clinic, or hospital.

— Apprise the Social Work Department Chair of the case on a regular/continuing basis.

— Act as case manager in gathering and sharing information with members of the support team.

— Establish contact with the hospital, physician or clinic providing service to the student.

— If the parents/guardians do not follow up with a referral within 24 hours, they will be informed by the social worker that the school is required to file a report with the Illinois Department of Children and Family Services. The report will be filed by the Assistant Principal for Student Services or the Dean of Students.

To those not suffering from depression or another mental illness, suicide is fundamentally an incomprehensible act - but for others it is all too real, and it claims the lives of some 30,000 Americans each year: people of every age, both men and women, within every group of population. The World Bank/World Health Organization-sponsored, Global Burden of Disease study reveals that suicide was the 9th leading cause of death among developed nations in 1990. What happens to these people? How do the neurochemicals and electrical impulses that account for the function of one's brain translate into a decision about death over life? Do the methods and messages of media contribute as precipitants of suicide, or are they potentially useful tools in its prevention?

Studies from the U.S., Finland, Sweden, and the U.K., all find that 90 percent of people who kill themselves have depression or another diagnosable mental or substance abuse disorder. From studies of the prevalence of depression - that is, the number of new and existing cases of depression over a given period of time - and data on the treated prevalence of depression, as many as one-third to a half of those individuals with depression who die by suicide likely are undiagnosed or are not receiving adequate and appropriate treatment for this potentially lethal disorder.

Although clinical depression, high rates of suicide also are associated with bipolar disorder, or manic depressive illness, with schizophrenia, and with other mental disorders. Estimates of the number of suicide victims who have had psychiatric treatment in their lifetimes range from 30 to 75 percent. These estimates vary depending on gender, age, their primary psychiatric illness, and where these people lived. A smaller group, 20 to 45 percent, was receiving psychiatric treatment at the time of their deaths that, for many was inadequate.

Some suicide victims who were not receiving psychiatric treatment were in contact with primary health care providers. This is particularly true for elderly persons who committed suicide; studies have shown that 70 percent of these individuals were in contact with a primary care provider within a month of their suicide. Suicide is always tragic; but because it is, potentially preventable through timely recognition and treatment of mental illness, the tragedy is compounded.

Adult Suicide

Most of the prior and current research on suicide

prevention in adults has focused on those with the highest risk of suicide - those who have made repeated suicide attempts. A few clinical research groups in the U.S., Europe, and Australia have evaluated interventions that include both medications and psychotherapy, but many of the studies did not have adequate numbers of patients to determine with any degree of certainty whether the intervention was truly effective. Fortunately, increasing numbers of researchers are becoming interested in developing treatments for such high-risk patients.

Adults in the treatment system who report high rates of suicide attempts include women with borderline personality disorder; men and women with depression who also abuse drugs or alcohol; and men and women with bipolar depression.

Up to two thirds of all patients who commit suicide have seen a physician in the month before their death. However, in few adult suicide victims is a mental disorder detected, and among those, treatment is usually inadequate. Training health care professionals, particularly those in the primary care sector, to treat recognize and treat or refer mental disorders appropriately is an urgent order of business if we are to reduce suicides. No less important - and, again, a challenge to the Nation that Dr. Satcher issues most compellingly in the Surgeon General's Report on Mental Health, is to combat the stigma attached to mental disorders and to encourage persons to seek treatment for mental disorders.

Older Adults Suicide

Among older adults - and, particularly, among older white males - late onset depression is the mental disorder most commonly associated with suicide. This form of depression, which typically is uncomplicated by substance abuse, is among the more readily treatable depressive disorders. Yet older persons at risk for suicide, like the majority of older adults in this country, tend not to seek mental health treatment. Rather, most have seen their primary care provider within the month, if not the week, of their death.

Youth Suicide

In the area of school-based suicide awareness programs, describing suicide and its risk factors, some curricula may have the unintended effect of suggesting that suicide is an option for young people who have some of the risk factors and in that sense "normalize" it . Many school districts, worried about liability issues, are purchasing suicide counseling packages from entrepreneurs seeking "quick fixes" to prevent suicides.

There are a number of prevention approaches that are less likely to have negative effects, and to have positive outcomes beyond that of reducing risk for suicide. One approach is to promote overall mental health among school-aged children by addressing early risk factors for depression, substance abuse and aggressive behaviors. In addition to the potential for saving lives, many more youth benefit from overall enhancement of academic performance and healthy peer and family relationships.

A second approach is to detect youth most likely to be suicidal by identifying those who have depression and/or substance abuse, combined with serious behavioral problems. Events such as recent tragic shootings in schools and other settings that capture public attention and concern are not typical of youth or adult violence, including suicide, but have focused the nation's attention on these important issues. By focusing research attention on high-risk groups, researchers have learned much about depression, substance abuse and frequently co-occurring aggressive and violent behavior.

Studies have shown that all of these problems share similar risk factors and processes - that is, the same experiences and influences act to increase risk for these problems. One might reason that comprehensive programs designed to reduce these risks also will reduce the often tragic outcomes, including suicide, that often are associated with such problems. Community efforts, involving parents, school systems, law enforcements officials, and other resources must communicate and work together to provide supportive, seamless treatment for youth with mental disorders.

School Intervention to Youth Suicide

Too many young people are not very happy. This is quite understandable among those living in economically impoverished neighborhoods where daily living and school conditions frequently are horrendous. But even youngsters with economic advantages too often report feeling alienated and lacking a sense of purpose. Youngsters who are unhappy usually act on such feelings. Some do so in "internalizing" ways; some "act out;" and some respond in both ways at different times. The variations can make matters a bit confusing. Is the youngster just sad? Is s/he depressed? Is this a case of ADHD?

Individuals may display the same behavior and yet the causes may be different and vice versa. And, matters are further muddled by the reality that the causes vary. The causes of negative feelings, thoughts, and behaviors range from environmental/system deficits to relatively minor group/individual vulnerabilities on to major biological disabilities (that affect only a small proportion of individuals). It is the full range of causes that account for the large number of children and adolescents who are reported as having psychosocial, mental health, or developmental problems. In the USA, estimates are approaching 20 percent (11 million).

Recent highly publicized events and related policy initiatives have focused renewed attention on youth suicide, depression, and violence. Unfortunately, such events and the initiatives that follow often narrow discussion of causes and how best to deal with problems. Shootings on campus are indeed important reminders that schools must help address violence in the society. Such events, however, can draw attention away from the full nature and scope of violence done to and by young people.

Similarly, renewed concern about youth suicide and depression are a welcome call to action. However, the actions must not simply reflect biological and psychopathological perspec- tives of cause and correction. The interventions must also involve schools and communities in approaches that counter the conditions that produce so much frustration, apathy, alienation, and hopelessness. This includes increasing the opportunities that can enhance the quality of youngsters' lives and their expectations for a positive future.

Violence

Violence toward and by young people is a fact of life. And, it is not just about guns and killing. For schools, violent acts are multifaceted and usually constitute major barriers to student learning. As Curcio and First note: Violence in schools is a complex issue. Students assault teachers, strangers harm children, students hurt each other, and any one of the parties may come to school already damaged and violated [e.g., physically, sexually, emotionally, or negligently at home or on their way to or from school]. The kind of violence an individual encounters varies also, ranging from mere bullying to rape or murder.

Surveys show that in some schools over 50% of the students have had personal property taken (including money stolen or extorted). Before recent campaigns for safe schools, one survey of 6th and 8th graders in a poor urban school found over 32% reporting they had carried a weapon to school-often because they felt unsafe.

Suicide and Depression

In the Surgeon General's Call to Action to Prevent Suicide 1999, the rate of suicide among those 10-14 years of age is reported as having increased by 100% from 1980-1996, with a 14% increase for those 15- 19. (In this latter age group, suicide is reported as the fourth leading cause of death.) Among African- American males in the 15-19 year age group, the rate of increase was 105%. And, of course, these figures don't include all those deaths classified as homicides or accidents that were in fact suicides.

Why would so many young people end their lives? The search for answers inevitably takes into the realm of psychopathology and especially the arena of depression. As we become sensitive to symptoms of depression, it is essential to differentiate common-place periods of unhappiness from the syndrome that indicates clinical depression. We must also remember that not all who commit suicide are clinically depressed and that most persons who are unhappy or even depressed do not commit suicide.

As the National Mental Health Association cautions: "Clinical depression goes beyond sadness or having a bad day. It is a form of mental illness that affects the way one feels, thinks, and acts." And, it does so in profound and pervasive ways that can lead to school failure, substance abuse, and sometimes suicide. Numbers for depression vary. The National Institute of Mental Health's figure is 1.5 million children and adolescents. The American Academy of Child and Adolescent Psychiatry estimates 3.0 million.

Variability in estimates contributes to appropriate concerns about the scope of misdiagnoses and misprescriptions. Such concerns increase with reports that, in 1998, children 2-18 years of age received 1.9 million prescriptions for six of the new antidepressants and about a third of these were written by nonpsychiatrists- generally pediatricians and family physicians. This last fact raises the likelihood that prescriptions often are provided without the type of psychological assessment generally viewed as necessary in making a differential diagnosis of clinical depression.

Instead, there is overreliance on observation of such symptoms as: persistent sadness and hopelessness, withdrawal from friends and previously enjoyed activities, increased irritability or agitation, missed school or poor school performance, changes in eating and sleeping habits, indecision, lack of concentration or forgetfulness, poor self-esteem, guilt, frequent somatic complaints, lack of enthusiasm, low energy, low motivation, substance abuse, recurring thoughts of death or suicide.

Clearly, any of the above indicators is a reason for concern. However, even well trained professionals using the best available assessment procedures find it challenging to determine in any specific case

— the severity of each symptom (e.g., when a bout of sadness should be labeled as profoundly persistent, when negative expectations about one's future should be designated as "hopelessness"),

— which and how many symptoms are transient responses to situational stress, and

— which and how many must be assessed as severe enough to warrant a diagnosis of depression.

Wisely, the Surgeon General's report on suicide stresses the linkage among various problems experienced by young people. This point has been made frequently over the years, and just as often, its implications are ignored. One link is life dissatisfaction. For any youngster and among any group of youngsters, such a state can result from multiple factors. Moreover, the impact on behavior[7] and the degree to which it is debilitating will vary considerably. And, when large numbers are affected at a school or in a neighborhood, the problem can profoundly exacerbate itself. In such cases, the need is not just to help specific individuals but to develop approaches that can break the vicious cycle. To do so, requires an appreciation of the overlapping nature of the many "risk" factors researchers find are associated with youngsters' behavior, emotional, and learning problems.

General Guidelines for Prevention

Various efforts have been made to outline guidelines for both primary and secondary (indicated) prevention. A general synthesis might include:

— Systemic changes designed to both minimize threats to and enhance feelings of competence, connectedness, and self-determination (e.g., emphasizing a caring and supportive climate in class and school-wide, personalizing instruction). Such changes seem easier to accomplish when smaller groupings of students are created by establishing smaller schools within larger ones and small cooperative groups in classrooms.

— Ensure a program is integrated into a comprehensive, multifaceted continuum of interventions.

— Build school, family, and community capacity for participation.

— Begin in the primary grades and maintain the whole continuum through high school.

— Adopt strategies to match the diversity of the consumers and interveners (e.g., age, socio economic status, ethnicity, gender, disabilities, motivation).

— Develop social, emotional, and cognitive assets and compensatory strategies for coping with deficit areas.

— Enhance efforts to clarify and communicate norms about appropriate and inappropriate behavior (e.g., clarity about rules, appropriate rule enforcement, positive "reinforcement" of appropriate behavior; campaigns against inappropriate behavior).

Protective Factors and Building Assets

Those concerned with countering the tendency to overemphasize individual pathology and deficits are stressing resilience and preventive factors and developing approaches designed to foster such factors. The type of factors receiving attention is exemplified by the following list:

Community and School

— Clarity of norms/rules about behavior (e.g., drugs, violence)

— Social organization (linkages among community members/capacity to solve community problems)

— Laws and consistency of enforcement of laws and rules about behavior (e.g., limiting ATOD, violent behavior)

— Low residential mobility

— Low exposure to violence in media

— Not living in poverty

Family and Peer

— Parental and/or sibling negative attitudes toward drug use

— Family management practices (e.g., frequent monitoring & supervision/consistent discipline practices)

— Attachment/bonding to family

— Attachment to prosocial others

Individual Factors

— Social & emotional competency

— Resilient temperament

— Belief in societal rules

— Religiosity

— Negative attitudes toward delinquency

— Negative attitudes toward drug use

— Positive academic performance

— Attachment & commitment to school

— Negative expectations related to drug effects

— Perceived norms regarding drug use and violence

The focus on protective factors and assets reflects the long-standing concern about how schools should play a greater role in promoting socio-emotional development and is part of a renewed and growing focus on youth development. After reviewing the best programs focused on preventing and correcting social and emotional problems, a consortium of professionals created the following synthesis of fundamental areas of competence

Emotional

— identifying and labeling feelings

— expressing feelings

— assessing the intensity of feelings

— managing feelings

— delaying gratification

— controlling impulses

— reducing stress

— knowing the difference between feelings and actions

Cognitive

— self-talk-conducting an "inner dialogue" as a way to cope with a topic or challenge or reinforce one's own behavior

— reading and interpreting social cues-for example, recognizing social influences on behavior and seeing oneself in the perspective of the larger community

— using steps for problem-solving and decisionmaking for instance, controlling impulses, setting goals, identifying alternative actions, anticipating consequences

— understanding the perspectives of others

— understanding behavioral norms (what is and is not acceptable behavior)

— a positive attitude toward life

— self-awareness-for example, developing realistic expectations about oneself

Behavioral

— nonverbal-communicating through eye contact, facial expressiveness, tone of voice, gestures, etc.

— verbal-making clear requests, responding effectively to criticism, resisting negative influences, listening to others, helping others, participating in positive peer groups

Initiatives focusing on resilience, protective factors, building assets, socio-emotional development, and youth development all are essential counter forces to tendencies to reduce the field of mental health to one that addresses only mental illness.

System Change

When it is evident that factors in the environment are major contributors to problems, such factors must be a primary focal point for intervention. Many aspects of schools and schooling have been so-identified. Therefore, sound approaches to youth suicide, depression, and violence must encompass extensive efforts aimed at systemic change. Of particular concern are changes that can enhance a caring and supportive climate and reduce unnecessary stress throughout a school. Such changes not only can have positive impact on current problems, they can prevent subsequent ones.

Caring has moral, social, and personal facets. From a psychological perspective, a classroom and schoolwide atmosphere that encourages mutual support and caring and creates a sense of community is fundamental to preventing learning, behavior, emotional, and health problems. Learning and teaching are experienced most positively when the learner cares about learning, the teacher cares about teaching, and schools function better when all involved parties care about each other. This is a key reason why caring should be a major focus of what is taught and learned.

Caring begins when students first arrive at a school. Schools do their job better when students feel truly welcome and have a range of social supports. A key facet of welcoming is to connect new students with peers and adults who will provide social support and advocacy. Over time, caring is best maintained through personalized instruction, regular student conferences, activity fostering social and emotional development, and opportunities for students to attain positive status. Efforts to create a caring classroom climate benefit from programs for cooperative learning, peer tutoring, mentoring, advocacy, peer counseling and mediation, human relations, and conflict resolution.

Clearly, a myriad of strategies can contribute to students feeling positively connected to the classroom and school. Given the need schools have for home involvement, a caring atmosphere must also be created for family members. Increased home involvement is more likely if families feel welcome and have access to social support at school. Thus, teachers and other school staff need to establish a program that effectively welcomes and connects families with school staff and other families in ways that generate ongoing social support. And, of course, school staff need to feel truly welcome and socially supported.

Rather than leaving this to chance, a caring school develops and institutionalizes a program to welcome and connect new staff with those with whom they will be working. Why should schools get involved? "Children are...much more likely to come into contact with potential rescuers in the school than they are in other community settings. This is especially true for younger children, who cannot move freely in the community.

In many instances, the child's problems, particularly those related to academics or the peer group, are more evident in the school setting than they are in the home...Further, the characteristic problems of a broken home or dysfunctional family, while not necessarily a direct cause of suicidal behavior, reduce the possibility of rescue in that setting."

According to Shaffer, Garland, Gould, Fisher, and Trautman, school-based suicide prevention programs tend to have the following goals in common:

— Heighten awareness of the problem

— Promote case finding (i.e., teaching teachers and especially other students to identify those who are at risk; increase disclosure of suicidal ideation by decreasing stereotypes that may cause stigma

— Provide staff and students with information about mental health resources-specifically how they operate and how they can be accessed

— Improve teenagers' coping abilities by training in stress management or coping strategies

A distinction is usually drawn between primary prevention which is aimed at the entire population, and secondary prevention which is aimed at those individuals who are at risk.

Primary Prevention: School personnel may work with the entire student body on suicide prevention by routinely including units on this topic in the curriculum at various levels, particularly in secondary schools; or they may institute discussions or modules at a time when there is some currency to the topic. Examples of opportune times are when a child in the school has committed suicide or made an attempt and has come to the notice of the student body at large. Other opportunities for primary prevention may be stimulated by the airing of television programs or movies which become popular and are seen by large numbers of students in a school. Primary prevention is usually accomplished in group settings using pre-planned curriculum material.

Secondary Prevention: Working with students who are at risk of attempting suicide constitutes secondary prevention. The individual most at risk is one who has attempted suicide in the past, but other students experiencing loss or shame are also at risk. Secondary prevention is likely to occur in individual or small group sessions and takes place as needed when risk factors build.

General Education Programs

There is a dearth of research evaluating youth suicide programs. Most of this research has focused on evaluating general education programs. In these programs, students are generally taught about suicide facts (and dispel myths), warning signs and risk factors, and provided information about mental health resources should they or one of their peers become suicidal. A small handful of general education programs focus on coping skills to deal with stressful situation. On average, these programs last 2 hours and have typically been integrated into the curricula of health classes.

The research findings regarding the efficacy of these programs have been mixed. First, some researchers have found that students tend to already be fairly knowledgeable about warning signs and youth suicide. Nevertheless, many studies have found increases in knowledge about facts and warning signs of suicide after completing general education programs compared to control group students. Moreover, students who participated in these programs tend to know more about mental health referral sources than their control group counterparts. A few studies have found positive changes in self-reported attitudes about coping skills in reaction to stress, hopelessness, and depression.

Despite these potential benefits, research suggests that general education programs may not be as effective as school personnel and mental health professionals would hope. For instance, many studies have found that while general education programs may increase students' general knowledge about suicide and warning signs, they do little to change students' attitudes about suicide and help-seeking behaviors. This finding has held despite efforts such as using better trained instructors or more sensitive instruments. Furthermore, researchers have primarily examined suicide knowledge and attitudes and have not looked at actual behaviors. While there is little evidence, in general, for increases in suicidal behavior or ideation in participants of general education programs, at least one large study found disconcerting iatrogenic effects of these programs on students who are at risk for suicide.

More specifically, it found that those students who reported a previous suicide attempt tended to not find the program helpful. Moreover, a greater proportion of previous attempters who had completed the program, compared to attempters who had not experienced the program, reported that they would not want to reveal suicidal ideation to others, believed that they could not be helped by a mental health profession, and stated that suicide was a reasonable solution to their problems .

Thus, according to the CDC , "Person's considering school-based general suicide education as a prevention strategy should also recognize that not all curricula are necessarily well-conceived. Some curricula are quite sensational, and thus may foster psyched contagion. Other curricula tend to 'normalize' suicide in a manner that some researchers fear will promote suicidal thinking by lessening whatever protective effects may derive from the social 'taboo' associated with suicide. Still other curricula inadvertently provide teens with clear 'how-to' instructions for committing suicide..."

Intervention can take many forms and should throughout the different stages in the process. Prevention includes education efforts to alert students and the community to the problem of teen suicidal behavior. Intervention with a suicidal student is aimed at protecting and helping the student who is currently in distress. Postvention occurs after there has been a suicide in the school community. It attempts to help those affected by the recent suicide. In all cases it is a good idea to have a clear plan in place in advance. It should involve staff members and administration. There should be clear protocols and clear lines of communication. Careful planning can make interventions more organized, and effective.

Prevention often involves education. This may be done in a health class, by the school nurse, school psychologist, guidance counselor or outside speakers. Education should address the factors that make individuals more vulnerable to suicidal thoughts. These would include depression, family stress, loss, and drug abuse. Other interventions may also be helpful. Anything that decreases drug and alcohol abuse would be useful. A study by Rich et al found that 67% of completed youth suicides involved mixed substance abuse. PTA meetings family spaghetti dinners can draw in parents so that they can be educated about depression and suicidal behavior. "Turn off the TV Week" campaigns can increase family communication if the family continues with the reduced TV viewing.

Parents should be educated about the risk of unsecured firearms in the home. Peer mediation and peer counseling programs can make help more accessible. However, it is critical that students go to an adult if serious behaviors or suicidal issues emerge. Outside mental health professionals can discuss their programs so that students can see that these individuals are approachable.

School Based Suicide Prevention Programs

A clear conceptual basis gives us the rationale for choosing a particular prevention strategy for a particular problem, with a particular population, in a particular setting. Part of the effort to build the conceptual base for prevention in general has resulted in typology intended to clarify prevention methodology which included:

1. Universal interventions, which are directed at an entire population rather than selected subpopulations or individuals.

2. Selective interventions, which are targeted to subpopulations that are characterized by shared exposure to some epidemiologically determined risk factor(s).

3. Indicated interventions are targeted to specific individuals who are already preclinical levels of a disorder and who have been identified through screening procedures.

Universal Suicide Prevention Approaches

The goal of universal approaches is to raise the overall supportiveness and responsiveness of the at risk youths' environment. The role of the school is seen as critical, but limited. All schools are not assumed to possess the resources to treat suicidal or emotionally disturbed students. They can enhance their capacity to identify and get help for these students as part of their mandate to socialize and protect their students. The overall goals of the universal program are to increase the likelihood that school gatekeepers (administrators, faculty, and staff) and peers who come into contact with at-risk youth can more readily identify them, provide an appropriate initial response to them, will know how to obtain help for them, and are consistently inclined to take such action.

Some longitudinal research indicates that the presence of protective factors may have a stronger influence on the likelihood that risk behaviors will occur than the presence of risk factors. These protective factors include personal characteristics such as social problem solving competencies; and, environmental characteristics such as contact with a caring adult and a school climate that promotes students' involvement, contribution, and sense of connection with their school. One caveat concerning resilient youth is in order. Research indicates that youth who come from high risk environments and yet do well in school and peer relations still evidence a greater prevalence of anxiety and depression than peers who do not come from such environments. Anxiety and depression are significant risk factors for suicide, and these internalizing disorders are more likely to go undetected than the externalizing behaviors.

While subgroups that are at greater risk for suicide will by definition be exposed to universal programs, these programs are aimed more at their peers and may not be of sufficient dosage or focus to affect specific vulnerable subpopulations such as disenfranchised or depressed students.

Some of these students may become known to school officials, particularly if school personnel and parents are educated to identify troubled students before they make overt statements or attempts. Thus gatekeeper training is a common selective program that has shown promise for increasing identification and referral. There is some evidence that students are more likely to use telephone crisis and referral services because they are anonymous, and don't require fees, transportation, or appointments. Publicizing these services (e.g. through wallet cards continuously available throughout the school) and linking them to established screening teams can facilitate contact with at risk youth. However, these services are still underutilized by males.

Indicated Suicide Prevention Programs

The goal of indicated programs is to reduce the incidence of suicidal behaviors among students who already display risk factors or early warning signs associated with suicide such as frequent suicidal thoughts, previous attempts, depression, or substance abuse. Indicated programs require the presence in schools of individuals who are trained to screen students and to provided the indicated programs.

School faculty or special services staff such as guidance counselors can be trained to provide the programs, but professionals such as psychologists or social workers would have to conduct the screening. There are a growing number of school-linked services (community gatekeepers who provide assessment and counseling services on site) and school based service centers or clinics that can house indicated interventions.

The overall goals of indicated programs are to identify at risk students, preferably through existing school procedures, and provide them with accessible, brief interventions that include support, skill training, and opportunities to bond with the school and maintain contact with a caring adult.

Comprehensive Programs

Comprehensive programs are multilevel, multicomponent interventions that include the following components, usually implemented in this order:

— Administrative consultation to ensure that policies and procedures for responding to at risk students, attempts, and completions are in place; and to ensure that community linkages exist for close coordination of referrals to, and return of students from, community gatekeepers.

— School gatekeeper training for all faculty and staff on the identification of, initial response to, and effective referral of troubled and at risk students. This sometimes includes the establishment of in school crisis response teams made up of faculty, staff, and administrators.

— Parent training covering similar material as the school gatekeeper training, as well as means restriction strategies.

— Community gatekeeper training that incorporates policies and procedures for effective response and coordination with schools and families. This sometimes includes training in the treatment of depressed and suicidal adolescents. Community crisis teams and media campaigns have also been implemented.

— Student classes usually consist of 4 to 5 class periods included in the health curriculum. Classes include a variety of media, and involve students in discussions and roleplays to prepare them to recognize and respond to troubled peers, and to destigmatize seeking adult help.

— Postvention interventions that are provided by external consultants to schools and communities in which a suicide completion or serious attempt has occurred. These interventions consist of standard steps designed to process faculty, student, and community reactions to the event; facilitate grief work; and, prevent imitative acts among identified vulnerable peers.

Assessing Suicide Risk

Identifying and Addressing Risk

It is difficult to identify particular individuals at greatest risk for suicidal behaviors or completed suicide. Measures to screen the general population for suicide risk lack the precision needed to identify in advance only those people who eventually would die by suicide. Because suicide screening in the general population currently is not feasible, it is especially important for suicide prevention programs to include broader approaches that benefit the whole population as well as efforts focused on smaller, high-risk subgroups that can be identified. Within those subgroups, a different approach to screening -screening programs for specific disorders, like depression, that are associated with suicide- can be used to identify and direct people to highly effective treatments that may lower their risk of suicide.

Often, the suicide prevention efforts in place are directed primarily at improving clinical care for the individual already struggling with suicidal ideas or the individual requiring medical attention for a suicide attempt. Suicide prevention also demands approaches that reduce the likelihood of suicide before vulnerable individuals reach the point of danger. Applying the public health approach to the problem of suicide in the United States will maximize the benefits of efforts and resources for suicide prevention.

Suicide is a public health problem that requires an evidence-based approach to prevention. In concert with the clinical medical approach, which explores the history and health conditions that could lead to suicide in a single individual, the public health approach focuses on identifying and understanding patterns of suicide and suicidal behavior throughout a group or population. The public health approach defines the problem, identifies risk factors and causes of the problem, develops interventions evaluated for effectiveness, and implements such interventions widely in a variety of communities.

Although this description suggests a linear progression from the first step to the last, in reality the steps occur simultaneously and depend on each other. For example, systems for gathering information to define the exact nature of the suicide problem may also be useful in evaluating programs. Similarly, information gained from program evaluation and implementation may lead to new and promising interventions. Public health has traditionally used this model to respond to epidemics of infectious disease. During the past few decades, the model has also been used to address other problems that are likewise complicated and challenging to prevent, such as chronic disease and injury.

The Public Health Approach Applied to Suicide Prevention

The first step includes collecting information about incidents of suicide and suicidal behavior. It goes beyond simple counting. Information is gathered on characteristics of the persons involved, the circumstances of the incidents, events that may have precipitated the act, the adequacy of support and health services received, and the severity and cost of the injuries. This step covers the who, what, when, where, how, and how many of the identified problem.

The second step focuses on why. It addresses risk factors such as depression, alcohol and other drug use, bereavement, or job loss. This step may be used to define groups of people at higher risk for suicide. Many questions remain, however, about the interactive matrix of risk and protective factors in suicide and suicidal behavior and, more importantly, how this interaction can be modified.

The next step involves developing approaches to address the causes and risk factors that have been identified. Testing the effectiveness of each approach is a critical part of this step to ensure that strategies are safe, ethical, and feasible. Pilot testing, which may reveal differences among particular age, gender, ethnic and cultural groups, can help determine for whom a suicide prevention strategy is best fitted.

The final step is to implement interventions that have demonstrated effectiveness in preventing suicide and suicidal behavior. Implementation requires data collection as a means to continue evaluating effectiveness of an intervention. This is essential because an intervention that has been found effective in a clinical trial or academic study may have different outcomes in other settings. Ongoing evaluation builds the evidence base for refining and extending effective suicide prevention programs. Determination of an intervention's cost-effectiveness is another important component of this step. This ensures that limited resources can be used to achieve the greatest benefit.

As interventions for preventing suicide are developed and implemented, communities must consider several key factors. Interventions have a much greater likelihood of success if they involve a variety of services and providers. This requires community leaders to build effective coalitions across traditionally separate sectors, such as the health care delivery system, the mental health system, faith communities, schools, social services, civic groups, and the public health system. Interventions must be adapted to support and reflect the experience of survivors and specific community values, cultures, and standards. They must also be designed to benefit from multi-ethnic and culturally diverse participation from all segments of the community.

As it evolves, America's National Strategy for Suicide Prevention must recognize and affirm the value, dignity, and importance of each person. Everyone concerned with suicide prevention shares the responsibility to help change and eliminate the societal conditions and attitudes that often contribute to suicide. Individuals, communities, organizations, and leaders at all levels should collaborate in promoting suicide prevention. Final development of a National Strategy for Suicide Prevention and the success of these essential action steps ultimately rest with individuals and communities and institutions and policy makers across the United States.

Risk Factors

Understanding risk factors can help dispel the myths that suicide is a random act or results from stress alone. Some persons are particularly vulnerable to suicide and suicidal self-injury because they have more than one mental disorder present, such as depression with alcohol abuse. They may also be very impulsive and/or aggressive, and use highly lethal methods to attempt suicide. As noted above, the importance of certain risk factors and their combination vary by age, gender, and ethnicity.

The impact of some risk factors can be reduced by interventions (such as providing effective treatments for depressive illness). Those risk factors that cannot be changed (such as a previous suicide attempt) can alert others to the heightened risk of suicide during periods of the recurrence of a mental or substance abuse disorder, or following a significant stressful life event. Risk factors include:

— Previous suicide attempt

— Mental disorders - particularly mood disorders such as depression and bipolar disorder

— Co-occurring mental and alcohol and substance abuse disorders

— Family history of suicide

— Hopelessness

— Impulsive and/or aggressive tendencies

— Barriers to accessing mental health treatment

— Relational, social, work, or financial loss

— Physical illness

— Easy access to lethal methods, especially guns

— Unwillingness to seek help because of stigma attached to mental and substance abuse disorders and/or suicidal thoughts

— Influence of significant people- family members, celebrities, peers who have died by suicide- both through direct personal contact or inappropriate media representations

— Cultural and religious beliefs- for instance, the belief that suicide is a noble resolution of a personal dilemma

— Local epidemics of suicide that have a contagious influence

— Isolation, a feeling of being cut off from other people

Some lists of warning signs for suicide have been created in an effort to identify and increase the referral of persons at risk. However, the warning signs given are not necessarily risk factors for suicide and may include common behaviors among distressed persons, behaviors that are not specific for suicide. If such lists are applied broadly, for instance in the general classroom setting, they may be counterproductive.

In effect, indiscriminate suicide awareness efforts and overly inclusive screening lists may promote suicide as a possible solution to ordinary distress or suggest that suicidal thoughts and behaviors are normal responses to stress. Efforts must be made to avoid normalizing, glorifying, or dramatizing suicidal behavior, reporting how-to methods, or describing suicide as an understandable solution to a traumatic or stressful life event. Inappropriate approaches could potentially increase the risk for suicidal behavior in vulnerable individuals, particularly youth.

Protective Factors

Protective factors can include an individual's genetic or neurobiological makeup, attitudinal and behavioral characteristics, and environmental attributes.31 Measures that enhance resilience or protective factors are as essential as risk reduction in preventing suicide. Positive resistance to suicide is not permanent, so programs that support and maintain protection against suicide should be ongoing. Protective factors include:

— Effective and appropriate clinical care for mental, physical, and substance abuse disorders

— Easy access to a variety of clinical interventions and support for help seeking

— Restricted access to highly lethal methods of suicide

— Family and community support

— Support from ongoing medical and mental health care relationships

— Learned skills in problem solving, conflict resolution, and nonviolent handling of disputes

— Cultural and religious beliefs that discourage suicide and support self-preservation instincts

The risk factors that lead to suicide (especially mental and substance abuse disorders) and the protective factors that safeguard against it form the conceptual framework for the prevention recommendations developed and presented in this document and in the evolving National Strategy for Suicide Prevention.

Risk factors of Teenagers

Biological Factors

Genetics: Suicide may run in families. Studies have found that even after taking into account the increased rates of psychiatric disorders in the families of suicide attempters, the first-degree relatives were still more likely to attempt suicide compared to the relatives of controls. This indicates that aspects of suicidal behavior may be inherited independently from psychiatric disorders. Most likely multiple genes are involved in the inheritance of suicidal behavior.

Neurotransmitters: The neurotransmitter serotonin is strongly associated with suicidal behavior. Serotonin has also been linked to the control of impulsivity, aggression, and depression; factors that can contribute to suicidal behavior. Researchers have examined several genes linked to serotonin, but results have been inconsistent. As yet, there are no clinically useful biological markers for suicide risk.

Interventions

Hospitalization: There is no evidence-based data that psychiatric hospitalization prevents immediate or eventual suicide, despite overwhelming clinical consensus that immediate hospitalization is a critical component in preventing both adult and teenaged suicidal patients from completing suicide. Studies comparing the efficacy of hospitalization compared to home/outpatient treatment have found no significant differences.

Psychotherapy: No treatment program has demonstrated a reduction in subsequent attempts by adolescent suicide attempters. This may be due to a lack of established treatments with proven long-term efficacy for disorders such as conduct disorder and substance abuse. An additional problem is that adolescents are generally not compliant with psychiatric treatment. The recommended approach is conscientious clinical followup of teenagers to ensure that they are engaged in treatment. Unless the general practioner, internist, or pediatrician has particular training or expertise in suicide prevention, teenagers with suicidal ideation, multiple risk factors, or a suicide attempt should be referred for a complete mental health evaluation and careful treatment.

Pharmacotherapy: The selective serotonin reuptake inhibitor (SSRI) antidepressants unequivocally reduce symptoms of major depression and generalized anxiety in adults. It has been more difficult to demonstrate consistent effects among teenagers. Additionally, although antidepressants might be efficacious for depression, little evidence exists that antidepressants significantly lower suicide rates.

There is strong and conclusive evidence that in adults with bipolar disorder, lithium as a part of long-term treatment acts as a protective factor against suicidal behavior. Especially in later adolescence, bipolar illness has classic adult features (grandiosity, pressured speech, decreased sleep, agitation, intense irritability). However, much academic controversy exists about the identification of bipolar illness in very young adolescents and prepubertal children. More research is needed to determine whether lithium is also effective at reducing suicide risk in teenagers.

Community-based suicide prevention: There is limited empirical data on the measurable effects of school-based programs and hotline crisis services on suicidal behavior. The value of many programs remains untested.

Suicidal ideation can be a symptom of depression. At the same time, other symptoms of depression can serve as warning signs for suicidal ideation . Five or more of the following symptoms have been present during the same 2-week period and represent a change from previous functioning; at least one of the symptoms is either (1) depressed mood or (2) loss of interest or pleasure.

— depressed mood most of the day, nearly every day, as indicated by either subjected report (e.g., feels sad or empty) or observation made by others (e.g., appears tearful). In children and adolescents, can be irritable mood.

— markedly diminished interest or pleasure in all, or almost all, activities most of the day, nearly every day (as indicated by either subjective account or observation made by others)

— significant weight loss when not dieting or weight gain (e.g., a change of more than 5% of body weight in a month), or decrease or increase in appetite nearly every day. Note: In children, consider failure to make expected weight gains.

— insomnia or hypersomnia nearly every day

— psychomotor agitation or retardation nearly every day (observable by others, not merely subjective feelings of restless or being slowed down)

— fatigue or loss of energy nearly every day

— feelings of worthlessness or excessive or inappropriate guilt (which may be delusional) nearly every day (not merely self-reproach or guilt about being sick)

— diminished ability to think or concentrate, or indecisiveness, nearly every day (either by subjective account or as observed by others)

— recurrent thoughts of death (not just fear of dying), recurrent suicidal ideation without a specific plan, or a suicide attempt or a specific plan for committing suicide

Symptoms

Sadness, irritability, or a loss of interest in normally pleasurable activities is a common and normal response to disappointment, failure, or loss. Such mood changes only represent a problem if they persist more than a few days and if they represent intense distress or significantly impair the child's ability to function or relate to others at home, school, or play. It is recommended that assessment of suicidal ideation, plan, and intent be undertaken routinely when these symptoms are present. Children and adolescents may not present with sadness, but may report aches and pains, low energy, or moods such as apathy, irritability or even anxiety.

The mood disorders include major depressive disorder, dysthymic disorder, bipolar disorders, and cyclothymic disorder. To meet criteria for major depressive disorder, children must present with:

1) depressed or irritable mood, or

2) markedly diminished interest or pleasure in all, or almost all, activities.

Bereavement is an intense grief response after a major loss (e.g., death of parent) and is usually a normal reaction involving mood and sleep or appetite changes. When bereavement symptoms persist for longer than 2 months or are characterized by marked functional impairment, morbid preoccupation with worthlessness or suicidal ideation, major depressive disorder can be diagnosed.

Approximately one third of teenagers with depression receive treatment. This is particularly problematic given the recurrent nature of depressive episodes) the possibility of suicide, and the heightened risk of greater frequency and severity of depressive disorders in adulthood for patients with early onset (before 20 years of age). Risk factors include depressed parent(s), a strong family history of depression, anxiety disorder, alcoholism, family and marital discord, substance abuse, uncertainty about sexual orientation, and a history of previous depressive episodes. The presence of suicidal ideation, a history of suicide attempt(s), or suicidal behavior among family members or friends should trigger a prompt and thorough evaluation of suicide potential.

Symptoms of depression are more prevalent in adolescence than in younger children and the rise may be due to a function of puberty rather than chronological age. Depressive disorders become more frequent during adolescence with a possible parallel shift in the sex ratio from a male preponderance before puberty to a female preponderance after puberty. Immediate grief reaction's following bereavement tend to be milder and of a shorter duration in younger children compared with those in adolescence or adulthood.

In the 14- to 18-year-old age group, the 1-year total incidence of depressive disorders is estimated to be 7.7%; most cases meet the criteria for a major depressive disorder. Prevalence and incidence rates are approximately twice as high for girls as for boys; this gender difference appears to emerge at about 12 to 13 years of age. Depression is I V2 to 3 times more common among first-degree biological relatives of persons with major depressive disorder than in the general population.

7

Suicide Prevention and Control

According to WHO estimates approximately one million people are likely to commit suicide in the year 2000. Suicide is among the top 10 causes of death in every country, and one of the three leading causes of death in the 15 to 35-year age group. The psychological and social impact of suicide on the family and society is immeasurable. On average, single suicide intimately affects at least six other people. If a suicide occurs in a school or workplace it has an impact on hundreds of people.

The burden of suicide can be estimated in terms of DALYs (disability-adjusted life years). According to this indicator, in 1998 suicide was responsible for 1.8% of the total burden of disease worldwide, varying between 2.3% in high-income countries and 1.7% in low-income countries. This is equal to the burden due to wars and homicide, roughly twice the burden of diabetes, and equal to the burden of birth asphyxia and trauma.

Suicide and Mental Disorders

Suicide is now understood as a multidimensional disorder, which results from a complex interaction of biological, genetic, psychological, sociological and environmental factors. Research has shown that between 40% and 60% of people who commit suicide had seen a physician in the month prior to suicide; of these, many more had seen a general physician rather than a psychiatrist. In countries where the mental health services are not well developed, the proportion of people in suicidal crisis consulting a general physician is likely to be higher.

To identify, assess and manage suicidal patients is an important task of the physician, who has a crucial role in suicide prevention. Studies from both developing and developed countries reveal an overall prevalence of mental disorders of 80-100% in cases of completed suicide. It is estimated that the lifetime risk of suicide in people with mood disorders is 6-15%; with alcoholism, 7-15%; and with schizophrenia, 4-10%.

However, a substantial proportion of people who commit suicide die without having seen a mental health professional. Hence improved detection, referral and management of psychiatric disorders in primary care is an important step in suicide prevention. A common finding in those who commit suicide is the presence of more than one disorder. The common disorders occurring together are alcoholism and mood disorder (i.e. depression), and personality disorder and other psychiatric disorders.

Mood disorders

All types of mood disorders have been associated with

suicide. These include bipolar affective disorder, depressive episode, recurrent depressive disorder and persistent mood disorders (e.g. cyclothymia and dysthymia), which form categories F31-F34 in ICD-10. Suicide is therefore a significant risk in unrecognized and untreated depression. Depression has a high prevalence in the general population and is not recognized by many as a disease. It is estimated that 30% of patients seen by a physician are suffering from depression. Roughly 60% of those who do seek treatment initially contact a general practitioner. It is a special challenge for the physician to work with both physical disease and psychological disorders simultaneously. In many instances, depression is masked and patients present only with somatic complaints.

Common presenting symptoms of depression are:

— Tiredness

— Sadness

— Lack of concentration

— Anxiety

— Irritability

— Sleep disturbances

— Pain in different parts of the body.

These symptoms should alert the physician to the presence of depression and lead to an assessment of the suicide risk. Specific clinical features associated with increased risk of suicide in depression are :

— Persistent insomnia

— Self-neglect

— Severe illness (particularly psychotic depression)

— Impaired memory

— Agitation

— Panic attacks.

The following factors increase the risk of suicide in people with depression:

— Age below 25 years in men

— Early phase of the illness

— Abuse of alcohol

— Depressed phase of a bipolar disorder

— Mixed (manic-depressive) state

— Psychotic mania.

Depression is an important factor in suicide among both adolescents and the elderly but those with late onset of depression are at a higher risk. Recent advances in the treatment of depression are very relevant for suicide prevention in primary care. Education of the general practitioner in identifying and treating depression was found to reduce suicide in Sweden. Epidemiological data suggest that antidepressants reduce suicide risk among the depressed. The full therapeutic dose of medication should be continued for several months. In the elderly it may be necessary to continue treatment for two years after recovery. Patients on regular lithium maintenance therapy have been found to have lower suicide risk.

Alcoholism

Alcoholism (both alcohol abuse and dependence on alcohol) is a frequent diagnosis in those who have committed suicide, particularly in young people. There are biological, psychological and social explanations for the correlation between suicide and alcoholism. Specific factors associated with increased suicide risk among alcoholics are:

— Early onset of alcoholism
— Long history of drinking
— High level of dependence
— Depressed mood
— Poor physical health
— Poor work performance
— Family history of alcoholism
— Recent disruption or loss of a major interpersonal relationship.

Schizophrenia

Suicide is the largest single cause of premature death among schizophrenics. Specific risk factors for suicide are:

— Young unemployed male
— Recurrent relapses
— Fear of deterioration, especially in those of high intellectual ability
— Positive symptoms of suspiciousness and delusions.
— Depressive symptoms.

The suicide risk is highest at the following times:

— Early stages of the illness

— Early relapse

— Early recovery.

Suicide risk decreases with increasing duration of the illness.

Personality disorders

Recent studies on young people who committed suicide have shown a high prevalence (20-50%) of personality disorder. The personality disorders that are more frequently associated with suicide are borderline personality and antisocial personality disorders. Histrionic and narcissistic personality disorders and certain psychological traits such as impulsivity and aggression, have also been associated with suicide.

Anxiety disorders

Among anxiety disorders, panic disorder has been most frequently associated with suicide, followed by obsessive-compulsive disorder (OCD). Somatoform disorder and eating disorders (anorexia nervosa and bulimia) are also related to suicidal behaviour.

Suicide and Physical Disorders

Suicide risk is increased in chronic physical illness . In addition, there is generally an increased rate of psychiatric disorder, especially depression, in people with physical illness. Chronicity, disability and negative prognosis are correlated with suicide.

Neurological diseases

Epilepsy has been associated with increased suicide. The increase has been attributed to the increased impulsivity, aggressivity and chronic disability associated with epilepsy. Spinal and brain injuries also increase the risk of suicide. Recent studies have shown that after a stroke - particularly in the presence of posterior lesions, which cause greater disability and physical impairment - 19% of patients are depressed and suicidal.

Neoplasms

The risk of suicide is highest at the time of diagnosis and in the first two years of the terminal illness with an increase in risk in cases of progressive malignancy. Pain is a significant contributing factor to suicide.

HIV/AIDS

HIV infection and AIDS represent an increased risk of suicide in the young, with high suicide rates. The risk is greater at the time of confirmation of the diagnosis and in the early stages of the illness. Intravenous drug users are at still higher risk.

Other conditions

Other chronic medical conditions such as chronic renal disease, liver disease, bone and joint disorders, cardiovascular disease and gastrointestinal disorders are implicated in suicide.

Disabilities of locomotion, blindness and deafness can also precipitate a suicide. In recent years euthanasia and assisted suicide have become issues that may confront the physician. Active euthanasia is illegal in almost all jurisdictions, and assisted suicide is enmeshed in moral, ethical and philosophical controversy.

Suicide and Sociodemographic factors

Suicide is an individual act; however, it occurs in the context of a given society, and certain sociodemographic factors are associated with it.

Sex

In the majority of countries, more males commit suicide than females; the male/female ratio varies from country to country. China is the only country in which female suicides outnumber male suicides in rural areas and are approximately equal to male suicides in urbanareas.

Age

The elderly (above 65 years) and the younger (15-30 years) age groups are at increased risk of suicide. Recent data suggest an increase in suicide rates in middle-aged men.

Marital status

Divorced, widowed and single people are at increased risk of suicide. Marriage appears to be protective for males in terms of suicide risk but not significantly so for females.

Marital separation and living alone increase the risk of suicide.

Occupation

Certain occupational groups such as veterinary surgeons, pharmacists, dentists, farmers and medical practitioners have a higher risk of suicide. There is no obvious explanation for this finding, though access to lethal means, work pressure, social isolation and financial difficulties might be the reasons.

Unemployment

There are fairly strong associations between unemployment rates and suicide rates, but the nature of these associations is complex. The effects of unemployment are probably mediated by factors such as poverty, social deprivation, domestic difficulties and hopelessness. On the other hand, people with mental disorders are more likely to be unemployed than people in good mental health. At any rate, due consideration should be given to the difference in the significance of recent loss of employment and long-term unemployment: greater risk is associated with the former.

Rural/urban residence

In some countries suicides are more frequent in urban areas, whereas in others they occur more frequently in rural areas.

Migration

Migration - with its attendant problems of poverty, poor housing, lack of social support and unmet expectations - increases the risk of suicide.

Other social factors

Certain social factors, such as the ready availability of the means of committing suicide and stressful life events play a significant role in increasing the risk of suicide.

How to identify patients at sucidal behaviour

A number of clinically useful individual and sociodemographic factors are associated with suicide. They include:

— Psychiatric disorders (generally depression, alcoholism and personality disorders);

— Physical illness (terminal, painful or debilitating illness, AIDS);

— Previous suicide attempts;

— Family history of suicide, alcoholism and/or other psychiatric disorders;

— Divorced, widowed or single status;

— Living alone (socially isolated);

— Unemployed or retired;

— Bereavement in childhood.

If the patient is under psychiatric treatment, the risk is higher in:

— Those who have recently been discharged from hospital;

— Those who have made previous suicide attempts.

In addition, recent life stressors associated with increased risk of suicide include:

— Marital separation;

— Bereavement:

— Family disturbances;

— Change in occupational or financial status;

— Rejection by a significant person;

— Shame and threat of being found guilty.

The physician may be confronted with a variety of conditions and situations associated with suicidal behaviour. An elderly male, recently widowed, treated for depression, living alone, with a history of attempted suicide, and a young lady with a few scratches on the forearm whose boyfriend has left her are two contrasting examples. In reality, most patients fall between those two extremes and they may fluctuate from one category to the other.

When physicians have a reasonable indication that the patient could be suicidal, they face the dilemma of how to proceed. Some physicians are uncomfortable with suicidal patients. It is important for them to be aware of that feeling and to seek help from colleagues, and possibly. mental health professionals, when confronted with such patients. It is essential not to ignore or deny the risk.

If the physician decides to proceed, the first and most immediate step is mentally to allocate adequate time to the patient, even though many others may be waiting outside the room. By showing a willingness to understand, the physician starts to establish a positive rapport with the patient. Closed-ended and direct questions at the beginning of the interview are not very helpful. Remarks like "You look very upset; tell me more about it" are useful. Listening with empathy is in itself a major step in reducing the level of suicidal despair.

How to ask?

It is not easy to ask patients about their suicidal ideas. It is helpful to lead into the topic gradually. A sequence of useful questions is:

1. Do you feel unhappy and helpless?
2. Do you feel desperate?
3. Do you feel unable to face each day?
4. Do you feel life is a burden?
5. Do you feel life is not worth living?
6. Do you feel like committing suicide?

When to ask?

It is important to ask these questions:

— After a rapport has been established;

— When the patient feels comfortable about expressing his or her feelings;

— When the patient is in the process of expressing negative feelings.

The process does not end with confirmation of the presence of suicidal ideas. It continues with further questions aimed at assessing the frequency and severity of the idea and the possibility of suicide. It is important to know whether the patient has made any plans and has the means to commit suicide. If a patient mentions that the method planned is shooting, but has no access to a gun, the risk is lower.

However, if a patient has planned a method and is in possession of the means (e.g. pills), or if the proposed means are easily accessible, the suicide risk is higher. It is crucial for questions not to be demanding or coercive, but to be asked in a warm way showing the physician's empathy with the patient. Such questions might include:

- Have you made any plans for ending your life?
- How are you planning to do it?
- Do you have in your possession [pills / guns / other means]?
- Have you considered when to do it?

Management of Suicidal Patients

If a patient is emotionally disturbed, with vague suicidal thoughts, the opportunity of ventilating thoughts and feelings to a physician who shows concern may be sufficient. Nevertheless, an opportunity for further follow-up should be left open, particularly if the patient has inadequate social support. Whatever the problem, the feelings of the suicidal person are usually a triad of helplessness, hopelessness and despair. The three most common states are:

1. *Ambivalence.* The majority of suicidal patients are ambivalent till the very end. There is a see-saw battle between the wish to live and the wish to die. If the ambivalence is used by the physician to increase the wish to live, the suicide risk may be reduced.
2. *Impulsivity.* Suicide is an impulsive phenomenon and impulse by its very nature is transient. If support is provided at the moment of impulse, the crisis may be defused.
3. *Rigidity.* Suicidal people are constricted in their thinking, mood and action and their reasoning is dichotomized in terms of either/or. By exploring several possible alternatives to death with the suicidal patient, the physician gently makes the patient realize that there are other options, even if they are not ideal.

Enlisting support

The physician should assess the available support systems, identify a relative, friend, acquaintance or other person who would be supportive to the patient, and solicit that person's help.

Contracting

Entering into a "no suicide" contract is a useful technique in suicide prevention. Other people close to the patient can be included in negotiating the contract. The negotiation of the contract can promote discussion of various relevant issues. In the majority of instances patients respect the promises they give to a physician. Contracting is appropriate only when patients have control over their actions.

In the absence of severe psychiatric disorder or suicidal intent, the physician can initiate and arrange pharmacological treatment, generally with antidepressants, and psychological (cognitive behaviour) therapy. The majority of people benefit from continuing contacts; these should be structured to meet individual needs.

Except for the treatment of underlying diseases, few persons require support for longer than two or three months and the focus of the support should be providing hope, encouraging independence, and helping the patient to learn different ways of coping with life stressors.

Referral to Specialist Care

When to refer a patient Patients should be referred to a psychiatrist when they have:

- A psychiatric disorder;
- A history of a previous suicide attempt;
- A family history of suicide, alcoholism and psychiatric disorder;
- Physical ill-health;
- No social support.

How to refer

After deciding to refer a patient, the physician should:

- Take the time to explain to the patient the reason for the referral;

— Allay anxiety about stigma and about psychotropic medication;

— Make clear that pharmacological and psychological therapies are effective;

— Emphasize that referral does not mean "abandonment"

— Arrange an appointment with the psychiatrist;

— Allocate a time for the patient after his or her appointment with the psychiatrist;

— Ensure that the relationship with the patient continues.

When to hospitalize a patient

These are some of the indications for immediate hospitalization:

— Recurrent thoughts of suicide;

— High level of intent to die in the immediate future (the next few hours or days);

— Agitation or panic;

— Existence of a plan to use a violent and immediate method.

How to hospitalize the patient

— Do not leave the patient alone;

— Arrange for hospitalization;

— Arrange for transfer to the hospital by ambulance or the police;

— Inform the concerned authorities and family.

Suicide rates among young people in New Zealand are high by international comparison. In common with other countries around the world, youth suicide rates in this country have been increasing over the last three decades. There has been a dramatic increase in the amount of published research into the risk factors, for suicide among young people both in this country and over-seas. The amount of research addressing the identification and management of young people at highrisk of suicide has also increased.

Particular attention has focused on the ability of health professionals in primary care with regard to their gatekeeping role in determining access to specialist treatment services. A number of groups have specifically called for the improved recognition and management of suicidal young people by primary care practitioners in New Zealand. The patient groups included in the research and the countries in which the research have been based have been highly variable.

An appreciation of these trends is important in any assessment of the risk factors for suicidal behaviour and the subsequent identification in the clinical setting of those young people who are most at risk of this behaviour. Epidemiological information is presented to describe the prevalence of suicide, attempted suicide and suicidal ideation among young people.

Conceptual Model of Suicide Risk

There have been a number of perspectives on the risk factors for suicidal behaviour among young people. Two main models of suicide risk have emerged from a review of the literature. The first model considers that risk is largely confined to young people with recognisable mental disorders, and draws support from the high rate of mental illness found in numerous case control studies e.g. Brent et al. and the strong association between suicidal behaviour and mental disorders noted in the Christchurch-based cohort study. Suicide is a response to overwhelming and untenable life stress that could happen to any adolescent, and psychopathology is not the most important variable e.g. Garland et al., Rubenstein et al., Rich et al. Against this viewpoint is the consistent finding of a strong association between psychopathology and suicidal behaviour and the negative findings from several studies that have specifically examined the relationship between stress and suicidal behaviour e.g. Fremouw et al.

The two models of suicide risk are important in that they each prescribe widely diverse interventions to reduce the rate of suicide among young people. The stress model demands that population-based programmes should be delivered (often within schools) to better equip all young people with techniques to cope with stress, while government should provide more employment opportunities for young people. By contrast the mental illness model calls for the strengthening of health services and generally suggests that suicide preventive services would be more effective if they were targeted at young people with psychiatric morbidity.

A biopsychosocial model that accommodates both of these main theories of the development of suicidal behaviour. The risk factors for suicidal behaviour among young people into six broad domains of factors after Beautrais. These six domains are:

1. Demographic and social factors, which provide social contextual factors which, may influence both an individual's predisposition to suicidal behaviours and to the expression of these behaviours.
2. Family characteristics and childhood experiences, including impaired child-parent relationships, exposure to physical or sexual abuse, and family dysfunction, which may influence an individual's longer term vulnerability to psychiatric disorder and suicidal behaviour.
3. Personality factors and cognitive style (including sexual orientation), which may reflect individual variations in temperamental or related factors which may act to encourage the development of suicidal behaviours.
4. Genetic and biological factors, which may influence individual vulnerability to psychiatric disorder and risk of suicidal behaviour.
5. Psychiatric morbidity, notably affective disorders which are frequently precursors of suicidal behaviours.
6. Environmental factors, including stressful and adverse life events or the provision of models of suicide, which may play the role of precipitating suicidal behaviours or of encouraging the expression of these behaviours.

Suicidal behaviour in the context of a biopsychosocial model that considers an individual's risk of suicide results from a large number of factors which reflect biologic and genetic influences, social, family and environmental influences and individual personality and psychiatric illness factors. This model suggests that the development and expression of suicide risk is the result of a complex interplay between six inter-related domains of factors. The main corollary of this model is that attempts to prevent suicidal behaviour among young people can be based on interventions that are designed to reduce the influence of any of these six domains of factors either separately or in combination.

General Trends

During the period 1981-1989 the annual number 1 of youth suicides increased dramatically in New Zealand from 60 deaths in 1981 to 131 deaths in 1989. Between 1990-1993 the annual number of deaths has remained relatively stable. Provisional figures for 1994-1996 indicate that the number of young suicide victims has slightly increased. The rate 2 of suicide among youth in New Zealand has markedly increased between 1985 to 1996 from 12.6 cases per 100,000 in 1985 to 26.9 cases per 100,000 in 1996.

A review of suicide rates in New Zealand by age group found that much of the increase in suicide rates in the 1980s and early 1990s was due to a disproportionate rise in suicide for young people, especially men.

Gender

While male deaths continue to outnumber those among females, the number of female deaths has increased over the last three years (from 16 in 1993 to 38 in 1996).

Consequently, the ratio of male to female deaths has decreased from nearly 7:1 in 1991 to approximately 3:1 by 1996. Despite this trend the rate of suicide still remains significantly higher for males than females (19.6 per 100,000 in 1985 and 39.5 per 100,000 in 1996 for males compared to 5.1 per 100,000 in 1985 and 12.6 per 100,000 in 1996 for females). Conversely the rate of attempted suicide is

1 The number of youth suicide victims is the actual number of people who have died by suicide.

2 The rate of youth suicide is the frequency with which suicide occurs relative to the total number of people in the defined population (people aged 15-24 years). consistently higher for females at each age group compared to males.

Young, male, suicide victims in New Zealand continue to be primarily aged between 20-24 years. By contrast, the age distribution of female deaths among the young has changed between 1991-1995. In 1991, only 25% of female suicide victims under 25 years of age were in the 15-19 year old age range whereas the proportion in this age group had increased to nearly 40% by 1995. By 1996, the suicide rate among females in the 15-19 age group (16.2 per 100,000) was higher than the rate for females aged 20-24 (12.4 per 100,000). The male suicide rate in each age bracket remains higher than the corresponding rate for females. Although youth have the highest age specific death rates for suicide it should be remembered that most suicides (approximately two thirds) in New Zealand occur among people over the age of 24 years. Death by suicide before 15 years of age continues to be extremely rare in New Zealand.

Ethnicity

Maori rates of suicide before 1995 have been generally lower than non-Maori. However, by the early 1990s the suicide rate for Maori was similar to non-Maori (Skegg et al. 1995). This change was primarily due to a sharp increase in suicide rates among young Maori (especially those aged 15-24 years) between 1987-1991. Langford et al. (1998) has argued that the rising suicide rates among young Maori is a reflection of an increasingly de-cultured, colonised and detribalised group who have lost their traditional cultural supports.

In 1995 the method used for recording ethnicity for all mortality data changed from a system that was based on a biological definition of ethnicity (i.e. 50% or more ancestry) to one that determined ethnicity by self-identification. This method is compatible with the data used for the denominator in the calculation of population rates, namely that obtained by the census. This change in the method of recording mortality information means that it is not possible to accurately compare data from 1995 and earlier with that obtained in 1996 and subsequent years. Suicide among young Pacific Islanders appears to be uncommon, in 1996 four Pacific Island youths died by suicide.

The most frequently reported method of suicide used by both males and females in 1995 was hanging (56% of deaths for males and 65% for females). The proportion of deaths by hanging has markedly increased among females between 1991-1995. Much of the increase in female suicides between 1991-1996 has been attributed to an increase in the number of deaths by hanging.

Rates of suicide among young people are high in New Zealand by international comparison. In 1995, New Zealand had the highest rate of suicide among young women amongst all the OECD countries, and the second highest rate of suicide among males aged under 25 years (44.1 per 100,000 in New Zealand compared to 45.4 per 100,000 for Finland). New Zealand and Australia are the only OECD countries in which youth suicide rates are higher than the average suicide rate for the entire population.

There has been a consistent trend of rising youth suicide rates (especially among males) over the last 20 years among the OECD countries. England and Wales have recorded an increase in youth suicide rates between 1960-1990. In the United States, youth suicide rates have doubled between 1950 and 1993.

In Australia rates of suicide have increased between 1960-1990. A similar trend of increasing youth suicide rates, predominantly among young males, has also been noted in Canada and several European countries. Recent figures suggest that the suicide rate in several countries, including New Zealand may be plateauing or even beginning to decline.

There is no clear explanation of why youth suicide rates are increasing. While the results from some studies have indicated that mental illness rates (especially major episodes of depression) among young people may have been increasing, other studies have not found any such increase. Two population-based, time series studies both consistently found that an increase in the rate of youth suicide was strongly correlated with rises in unemployment along with some other environmental factors. However, time series analysis has a limited ability to exclude other confounding explanations for these associations.

Epidemiology of suicide attempts

The incidence or prevalence of suicide attempts in the population has been estimated by the number of hospital admissions in a community and by specific surveys. In 1996, 751 females (rate of 282 per 100,000) and 437 males (rate of 163 per 100,000) hospitalisations were made for attempted suicide in New Zealand. The age specific hospitalisation rate for attempted suicide is highest among males in the 20-24 year old age group, while the rate for females is highest for 15-19 year olds.

Consistent with the increase in the number of completed suicides by youth between 1960 and 1990, hospitalisations for attempted suicide have also increased in New Zealand and most other OECD countries. Estimates of attempted suicide that are based on only hospital data are likely to underestimate the true incidence of suicide attempts as many may not result in the person receiving medical attention. Evidence that hospitalisation data presents only the 'tip of the ice-berg' comes from several population-based surveys that have specifically surveyed young people about their history of suicide attempts and whether they subsequently sought medical attention.

Typically, these cross sectional studies have found that only about 1 in 4 adolescents who have made a suicide attempt ever obtained any medical care. The best estimates of the lifetime prevalence of suicidal attempts by young people come from studies that have included a random, population-based sample. Only three studies were found that have assessed the lifetime prevalence of suicidal attempts using such a sample. These three studies, despite the variation in the age at which the information was obtained and some differences in the definition of a suicide attempt, consistently found that approximately 3.5% of all adolescents had attempted suicide.

Supportive evidence for the conclusion that around 3% of people aged between 16-18 years would have previously attempted suicide at least once in their lifetime comes from four large school-based surveys conducted in the United States. These surveys were carried out among students while they were at school and it is possible that these adolescents would be less likely than young people who were no longer attending high school to have ever attempted suicide. Nevertheless these studies are informative because of their large size and because they interviewed a random sample of school students. These studies found that a higher percentage of students reported that they had made at least one suicide attempt (around 7%). At least part of the explanation for the higher lifetime prevalence of suicide attempts among school-based samples may relate to the lower response rates in these surveys compared to those that had used a community sample. It is possible that the students, who responded to the questionnaire, may have been more likely to have a history of suicidal behaviour.

The relative reliability of either method of information gathering among young people is not known, and it is possible that students may either over-report, or alternatively, more accurately state their actual history of suicidal behaviour when a questionnaire is used to collect the data. By contrast, estimates of the lifetime prevalence of a suicide attempt that have been undertaken on small and highly selected populations in different school settings have exhibited considerable variation in their results.

Kienhorst et al. found that only 2.2% of adolescents had ever attempted suicide, whereas Rubenstein et al. estimated that the lifetime prevalence was 20% in another group of high school students. Some of the difference in the results obtained by these studies might also be due to the small sample sizes that have been used in these analyses. Several studies have found that although male youths have higher rates of completed suicide, females are more likely to attempt suicide.

Several community based cohort and cross sectional studies have examined the lifetime prevalence of severe suicidal ideation using representative samples of patients based in several countries. A New Zealand study reported that 12% of a birth cohort by 16 years of age had experienced serious suicidal ideation. This study was well conducted and losses to follow-up were modest and did not appear to have any systematic differences from those for whom data was available. However, no information was included on the cause of death for the small number of the cohort who had died. The study found that 12% of young people by the age of 16 years had seriously contemplated suicide.

At least part of the variation in the prevalence of suicidal ideation is also due to differences in the definition of suicidal ideation that have been used in the different studies. When suicidal ideation was defined as subjects endorsing any statement that expressed a wish to die, 26% of the sample were considered to have experienced suicidal ideation. However, when more stringent criteria were used then the lifetime prevalence was only 6%.

Finally, Fergusson and Lynskey considered it was likely that significant under-reporting may have occurred in the responses to their study. Most of the other studies have also referred to the difficulties in gaining accurate and reliable information on the past thoughts of adolescents, especially in relation to suicidal ideation. Surveys of the point prevalence of suicidal ideation among young people have generally produced highly variable results, largely in relation to significant limitations associated with the research. Studies based on highly selected groups of young university students have reported that over 35% of subjects had experienced serious suicidal ideation over the preceding year.

While suicidal ideation among young people appears common in the community, there is some evidence that persistent suicidal ideation may be related to subsequent suicidal attempts or death by suicide. The presence of an underlying mental illness was identified as a common factor present among young people with persistent suicidal ideation and among those who subsequently made a suicide attempt after 18 months of follow-up. Few studies have consistently found that patients who have attempted suicide are at high-risk of subsequent death by suicide.

Approximately 0.5-1% will die each year by suicide. Unfortunately these studies have been characterised by several significant limitations. The studies were based on a small number of patients, all had high losses to follow-up e.g. Granboulan et al. 52% lost to follow-up, Kerfoot and McHugh 69% were untraceable after 7 years and their retrospective analyses cannot exclude bias as an explanation for their findings. The high level of attrition from follow-up is especially significant because it is likely that patients defaulting from follow-up may be more likely to experience a poor outcome.

The risk factors for suicidal behaviour among youth are multifactorial, complex and probably interrelated. Several broad domains of factors have emerged in reviews examining the risk factors for youth suicide. This review examines the risk factors for suicidal behaviour among youth under six general domains of factors: social/demographic risk factors, family characteristics and childhood experiences, personality traits/disorders and cognitive style, genetic/biological risk factors, psychiatric risk factors, and life events or stresses.

Domain 1: Social and demographic risk factors

Young people at highest risk of suicide, or attempted suicide, are characterised by their low socioeconomic status and poor educational backgrounds. Although studies examining the relationship between socioeconomic status (SES) and educational background have not all consistently found that low SES and poor educational achievement have been associated with an increased risk of suicidal behaviour among young people e.g. Pelkonen et al., relatively strong evidence of the association between these variables comes from several studies that have employed a prospective study design e.g. Fergusson and Lynskey and have been well conducted e.g. Beautrais et al, Fergusson and Lynskey or were based on a large sample size.

Domain 2: Family characteristics/childhood background

A large number of studies have found that young people with suicidal behaviours come from family backgrounds characterised by dysfunctional or difficult circumstances. Strong and consistent associations have been found between suicidal behaviour and parental psychopathology, poor interfamilial communication and parental separation.

Parental psychopathology

A strong association has been found between parental psychopathology (especially parental substance abuse, affective disorders, antisocial behaviours, a familial history of suicide) and an increased risk of suicidal behaviour among young people in a number of trials with a variety of study designs, and based in a number of countries e.g. Brent et al., Gould et al., Fergusson and Lynskey. However, it should be noted that although an increased familial aggregation of suicide and psychiatric illness has been demonstrated by these studies and familial transmission inferred this cannot be definitively concluded from these studies.

Familial transmission might involve environmental factors such as a life-long exposure to violence, poor intra-familial relationships and dysfunctional communication. Large, prospective twin studies would be best able to elucidate the relative effects of genetic and environmental influences on suicidal behaviour. However, the time required conducting these studies does make them problematic to undertake.

Parental loss

Most studies have consistently found that parental loss (usually by separation or divorce) was significantly associated with suicidal behaviour among young people. Parental discord has also been associated with youth suicide.

Poor parental care/relationship with children (not including overt abuse), poor family communication

Although most studies have reported that impaired parent-child relationships have been associated with suicidal behaviour among young people one cohort study failed to find any relationship between the variables. At least in part this inconsistency may relate to the different ways that parent child relationships have been assessed by various studies e.g. in Allebeck and Allgulander and the parental bonding index in the study by Martin and Waite. It is notable that studies that have used the same method of measuring the quality of the parent-child relationship have consistently identified that poor parental care was a factor that increased the risk of suicidal behaviour among young people e.g. pa-rental bonding index and the studies by Martin and Waite, Tousignant et al., Martin et al., Beautrais et al.

Physical/sexual abuse

A large number of studies have recorded an excess risk of suicidal behaviour among youths in relation to a history of past physical and/or sexual abuse. The study by Brent et al. was an exception, although this study did find that past abuse was related to suicidal behaviour the association did not reach statistical significance perhaps due to an inadequate sample size.

Studies in selected populations that have reviewed the relationship between suicidal behaviour and sexual/ physical abuse have also reported associations between these two variables in relation to homosexual or chemically dependent young people.

Domain 3: Personality and cognitive attiributes and sexual orientation

A number of studies have found associations between suicidal behaviour and several personality disorders or traits. In general the evidence for an association between personality disorders and suicidal behaviour is more robust than that available for a relationship between personality traits and suicidal behaviour among young people. Studies that have examined the association between personality traits and youth suicidal behaviour have usually had small sample sizes e.g. Brent et al. or have been unable to exclude bias as an explanation for any association e.g. Kashani et al.

The evidence for an association between certain cognitive styles and suicidal behaviour among young people is even weaker, while there is no consistent evidence of any relationship between sexual orientation and suicidal behaviour among young people.

The personality disorders have included antisocial, borderline and avoidance disorders, while the traits have included impulsivity, anger and aggressiveness or withdrawal. These personality disorders have in common symptoms of intense rage and impulsive behaviour.

Sexual orientation

It has been suggested that the stigmatisation of homosexual young people is associated with an increased risk of suicide particularly among gay men. Few studies have evaluated the risk of suicide among homosexual young people, and although one reported very high rates of suicidal behaviour among gay youths frequenting support groups or bars, the validity of this study's findings was limited by the lack of a community control group. Significantly, the study that included a more representative control group failed to find any increased risk of suicidal behaviour among homosexual young people.

Cognitive styles and suicidal behaviour

Cognitive styles (the way in which an individual perceives, mentally organises and understands life experiences) also appear to be related to the risk of suicidal behaviour although the relationship has been noted in a relatively small number of studies that have involved modest sample sizes. Tendencies to think in a relatively inflexible manner and poor problem solving ability have been related to suicidal behaviour. Finally, a negative or hopeless outlook has also been associated with suicidal behaviour.

Domain 4: Biological risk factors for suicidal behaviour among young poeple

There is some evidence that reduced levels of sero-tonergic activity exist in the brains of suicide victims and suicide attempters. There is also some evidence that altered serotonin levels and impulsivity or aggression may be linked, and it has been noted that these traits are also associated with suicidal behaviour. However, relatively little is known about the effects of serotonin and the relationship between the level of this compound (and its metabolites) and suicide. It is also unclear if levels of these compounds are related to the suicide behaviour or an underlying specific psychiatric disorder, especially depression.

Low serum cholesterol levels have been associated with suicide but recent data has not found any association between the variables. Several studies have found that suicidal behaviour is more common among young people with relatives who have exhibited suicidal behaviour. However, as discussed in the family characteristics domain it is unclear whether this increased risk of suicidal behaviour among the children of suicidal parents is due to a genetic or environmental cause. In addition, it is unclear from the research whether what is being transmitted is a biological predisposition to suicide or a biological vulnerability to the psychiatric disorders with which suicide is commonly associated.

Domain 5: Psychiatric morbidity as a risk factor for suicidal behaviour

Most studies of suicidal behaviour among young people have consistently reported that the majority of young people who die by suicide or make a serious attempt have a recognisable psychiatric disorder at the time of their attempt. Most commonly, these disorders are affective disorders, substance abuse and antisocial behaviours. The link between suicidal behaviour and depression is especially important because of the relatively high prevalence of depression. This link has been established from the results of numerous studies, based in a number of countries, and which have used two major study designs - prospective cohort studies and retrospective case control studies based on the psychological profiles of suicide victims. Although relatively few young people will have a psychotic disorder (such as schizophrenia), amongst the relatively small number with these severe mental illnesses the risk of suicide is very high.

Comorbid mental disorders

There is significant evidence that there is an increased risk of suicidal behaviour among those young people with comorbid psychiatric conditions (that is, the occurrence of more than one psychiatric condition at the same time. The increased risk may be directly proportional to the number of comorbid conditions.

Domain 6: Precipitating stressful events

A significant body of research has found that suicidal behaviour is often preceded by a stressful life event especially: an interpersonal conflict, loss, or legal/disciplinary problems. These events may act as a precipitant for suicidal behaviour in an adolescent who often may have other underlying risk factors. A well recognised problem with studying the relationship between life events and suicide is that either a suicide attempter's responses (or those of a victim's family) to questions about life events may be subject to bias. It is possible that mental illness may influence the reporting of life events among young people. In addition, it is also possible that a victim's family may recall more preceding stressful life events prior to a suicide in order to "make sense" of a tragic death.

The study by Beautrais et al. is notable because it purposely attempted to prevent bias by checking the data gathered from suicide attempters about recent stressful life events against separate reports obtained from significant other informants.

Although the risk factors have been presented separately they are interrelated and they operate in a complex manner over differing time periods in ways that are unique to individuals. For example, young people who are unemployed are also more likely to have a psychiatric illness, and also more likely to have socioeconomically disadvantaged families, that also have higher rates of parental psychopathology.

The findings from the study by Beautrais et al. clearly illustrate the complex relationships that exist between the risk factor domains. Beautrais et al. found that sociodemographic and family characteristic risk factors were related to environmental factors which were all related to the incidence of suicidal behaviour in young people. In addition, these same sociodemographic and family characteristic risk factors were related to psychiatric morbidity, which were all also related to suicidal behaviour. Finally, environmental and psychiatric risk factors were related to each other and also to the development of suicidal behaviour in young people.

Importance of Different risk Factor Domains

A number of studies have estimated the relative importance of the different domains of risk factors by univariate/multivariate analyses (based on cross sectional data), and by calculating the odds ratio or relative risk for adolescents who died by suicide, or suicide attempters, who were exposed to the risk factor in relation to those other adolescents who were not. The results of these analyses have consistently found that a concurrent mental illness, and in particular the presence of comorbid psychopathologies, are uniformly the most important risk factor.

Studies that have assessed the prevalence of diagnosable psychopathology among suicide victims by means of psychological autopsy investigations have consistently found that 80%-90% of victims had a psychiatric condition at the time of their death. Among these studies the presence of an affective disorder (43%-63% of victims) and substance abuse (26%-47% of victims) have been the most psychiatric diagnoses. Similarly studies that used a cohort design have also commonly found a statistically significant relationship between psychiatric morbidity and suicidal behaviour.

The two New Zealand-based studies that have presented an estimate of the size of the association between the different risk factors and suicidal behaviour have both consistently found that the odds ratio (or relative risk) was largest between the presence of various psychiatric disorders and suicidal behaviour. Although not as strong as the relationship between psychiatric morbidity and suicidal behaviour there is also consistent evidence that suicidal behaviour among young people is associated with the sociode-mographic and family characteristics/childhood experiences domain of risk factors. The evidence for the relationship between suicidal behaviours among young people and the personality traits/disorders/cognitive styles/sexual orientation or biological risk factor domains is generally less convincing.

Relationship between suicidal ideation and suicidal attempts

Studies that have addressed the relationship between suicidal ideation and suicidal attempts/acts have done so by an assessment of the similarities and differences between those subjects that either have, or have not, reported these factors. In community based studies those making attempts are characterised as having a greater burden of psychosocial risk factors for suicide (higher rates of psychiatric disorders, and greater socioeconomic and familial adversity). For example, in the study by Brent et al. suicide attempters and ideators shared similar risk factors except that there was a higher prevalence of the major risk factors e.g. depression, substance abuse and chronic family discord) among those young people who had attempted suicide.

However, in clinic based studies e.g. Kosky et al., Carlson and Cantwell those adolescents who have made attempts have generally not differed from those with suicidal ideation. It may be that patients in clinic settings have generally higher levels of psychopathology, and consequently differences between the two populations (if they exist) may therefore be obscured. Alternatively, this disparity might be explained by the cross sectional study designs that have generally been used to examine the relationship between ideation and suicide attempts.

A cross sectional study design is inherently unable to assess causality because the time sequence of any association cannot be ascertained. While it is possible that people with ideation are more likely to commit suicide it could also be true that those people who have attempted suicide might be more prone to ruminate about killing themselves. The only reliable method of ascertaining whether suicidal ideation is an accurate predictor of suicidal behaviour is to follow representative, population-based, samples of patients with and without suicidal ideation over a number of years to assess how many subsequently undertook suicidal behaviour. The only study that has used this type of methodology is the Christ-church-based prospective cohort study. The results of this study have been consistent with the continuum model, those young people that have reported suicidal ideation are most likely to subsequently attempt suicide when they have a greater burden of psychosocial risk factors especially psychiatric illness and a disadvantaged background.

The two most important corollaries of the continuum model are:

1. Young people most at risk of suicide can (to some extent) now be predicted. That is, in those individuals with suicidal ideation but no or few additional risk factors suicide is unlikely, and conversely, the highrisk adolescent is characterised by suicidal ideation and multiple risk factors.
2. Interventions that reduce the frequency and the effect of the underlying major risk factors will be the most effective at reducing the rate of suicide among young people.

The identification and assessment of suicide risk among young people. The management of suicidal young people and the prevention of suicidal behaviour among young people. One of the most difficult clinical problems facing the primary care practitioner is the prediction and prevention of youth suicide. The prevention of suicide depends on the early recognition of those young people who are most at risk of suicidal behaviour.

Uunder-Recognition of Both Suicide Risk and Mental Illness

Primary care professionals are centrally placed to recognise and initiate treatment for adolescents with mental illness. These professionals (principally GPs) have been recognised as the main gatekeeper through whom most adolescents will receive both the diagnosis and the treatment for their mental illness. However, research findings suggest that a considerable amount of mental illness and many suicidal young people were unrecognised by health professionals. Although adolescents with suicidal behaviour do frequently attend health professionals (usually GPs) around the time of their event, their elevated risk of suicide was frequently not recognised by the doctor.

Two communitybased surveys of adolescents by Velez and Cohen and Garrison et al. have both reported that only approximately 20-27% of adolescents who had attempted suicide subsequently received any medical attention. By contrast, a small case control study by Vassilas and Morgan found that suicidal young people prior to their attempt were no more likely than their non-suicidal peers to consult a GP. Three studies have reported that the elevated risk of suicide among adolescents who subsequently made an attempt within one month of attending a primary care physician was infrequently recognised by the doctors who had been consulted prior to the event.

Although the studies that have investigated the identification of suicide risk among adolescents do have a number of serious methodological limitations e.g. small numbers, retrospective design, reliance on case note based information their results are generally consistent with other research that has concluded that many episodes of mental illness (especially depression) among young people are also unrecognised by patients and professionals, and consequently are left untreated. Newman et al. found that

25% of a New Zealand based cohort did not seek medical care for their mental illness. Similarly, Lewinsohn in another community based survey found that only 23% of adolescents had received any treatment for their first episode of major depression.

Under-Recognition /Treatment of Mental Illnesss

The under recognition of mental illness implies that these conditions also remain under-treated in young people. The difficulty for adolescent people in obtaining treatment for their mental illness is concerning because evidence exists that the delayed treatment of mental illness in this age group can result in both immediate and long term harm to the individual, their families and society. The period between the onset of major mental illness and treatment can be characterised by severe behavioural disturbance, family distress and morbidity for the patient as well as their family and friends.

Helgason found in a prospective cohort study that better outcomes for adolescent patients were associated with those individuals who received earlier treatment for their first episode of serious mental illness. Early treatment has been associated with shorter inpatient care and fewer episodes of subsequent hospitalisation, and consequently less expensive treatment for adolescents with serious mental illnesses.

The possibility of underrecognition and under treatment of depression among young people is especially concerning because the condition is common and because the disorder can be readily treated with modern therapy. New Zealand based research has found that the prevalence of depression over a 12 month period may be as high as 16.7% for 18 year old adolescents.

Despite the high prevalence of depression among young people several (overseas based) studies have found that many episodes of depression were not recognised by primary care practitioners. The underrecognition of depression denies young people access to effective interventions that could treat their condition. Good evidence exists from randomised controlled trials that psychotherapeutic and pharmacological interventions are very effective at treating depression among young people.

There are a number of possible reasons for why mental illness and suicide attempts might frequently be left undiagnosed and untreated among adolescents. These reasons include difficulties with the recognition of mental disorders by professionals, parents, teachers, and among the teenagers themselves along with their peers. A number of the potential reasons have been presented in the literature, however it must be recognised that these possibilities have usually not received any evaluation and are often just based on the opinions of health professionals, and less frequently, adolescents.

Care for Adolescents

Many authors have addressed the need to reduce the barriers for young people to receiving both an appropriate diagnosis and the best treatment for their mental illness as well as the prevention of suicide among this age group. However, most of the literature that has been published has been based solely on the opinions of health professionals.

Practice based methods

Health professionals can help overcome many of the barriers that may prevent the adolescent from seeking care. For example, practitioners can ensure that their reception staff are aware of the importance of making adolescents feel welcome, and maintain flexibility with appointment times to accommodate adolescents while emphasising the confidential nature of all consultations. The waiting room should contain some posters, magazines and written material that are appropriate for adolescents. Cost savings from budget holding can be used by groups of GPs (or others) to target adolescents to receive free or subsidised services.

Improved specialist services for adolescent mental health and good communication between these services and primary care practitioners would also improve the access for young people to treatment for their mental illness. A public education campaign designed for adolescents, schools and parents to inform them that primary care providers are available, interested and capable of looking after the heath care needs of adolescents including their mental health could overcome some of the psychological barriers of these groups and improve access to care for young people.

Some adolescents may regard adults as incapable of understanding their world, considerable effort is required to engage these young people in a therapeutic relationship. An understanding of the essential physical, emotional and psychological changes that are part of adolescence has been cited by a number of experts as essential knowledge to underpin effective consulting with adolescents. These changes include issues associated with a process of forming a selfidentity and gaining autonomy.

The development of sexual identity and body image, establishing relationships with peers, and gaining respect for both others and themselves are all important tasks of adolescence. Recognition of these changes and the issues often associated with them (such as conflicts with parents and authority figures, concern with maintaining popularity with peers and frequent distress with relationship difficulties) can markedly improve an awareness and understanding of how a young person functions.

A number of specific techniques have been suggested as important to establish an effective therapeutic relationship with an adolescent. Better relationships between patient and practitioner have been associated with improved compliance among adolescents. Many of these techniques are not unique to consulting with adolescents although they may be of particular importance in dealing with people of this age group. These techniques are based on the opinion of expert practitioners:

Consultation techniques

— Treat the young person with respect and identify from the outset that they (and not their parents or teachers) are the patient - for example, when the patient is accompanied by his/her parents greet the young person before acknowledging the parents.

— Exhibiting friendliness, warmth and an interest in the activities and concerns of the adolescent are important.

— When the patient is escorted by friends or relatives the adolescent should be invited to be seen alone during the consultation. It may also be helpful, with the patient's consent, to separately interview the patient's parents (or other significant person) as well.

Several studies have found that there are significant discrepancies between the reports of adolescents and those of their parents with regard to the occurrence of episodes of mental illness e.g. Marttunen et al., Nelson et al., Newman et al.. People close to the individual can provide important information about any alterations in the behaviour of the patient, or changes in their relationships with the individual, while the patient can usually narrate their own historical account of their symptoms.

— It is important to clearly inform the adolescent of the confidential nature of the therapeutic relationship, which will be respected in all situations except an extreme emergency. However, it should also be explained that some information may be shared with other professionals to assist with the care of the patient and itemise what may be disclosed.

— Listen carefully, compliment the adolescent on their strengths and avoid arguments.

— Maintain an empathic nonauthoritarian attitude and involve the adolescent patient in the clinical decisionmaking. Compliance may be enhanced by sharing with the patient 'ownership' over the treatment plan and allowing them to shape it towards their lifestyle and beliefs. Sometimes it may be necessary to compromise from the ideal treatment in order to ensure a treatment plan that the adolescent will accept and follow.

— It is especially important to be clear and precise in communicating with an adolescent who may be suicidal, because they may often be confused or in a state of chaotic feelings in relation to a mental illness or recent stressful event.

— Ensure that the practitioner is relaxed with the adolescent and does not adopt a false persona. In particular, the practitioner should talk freely with the adolescent without falsely trying to adopt the adolescent's colloquialisms. By contrast, the use of professional jargon should also be avoided. Communication should therefore be at a level that the person can understand and frequent direct questioning of comprehension may be necessary.

— Ensuring that goals are clear and set in an immediate time frame is important. Adolescents do not respond well to distant and vague concepts such as the need to change their behaviour in order to prevent the development of a disease in the distant future.

— Involvement of family or peers in the treatment of an adolescents can help promote a support network to become established for the patient. The people in this network can provide emotional as well as practical support, for example by driving the patient to appointments or by acting as an advocate for the young person. Care must be exercised that consent is obtained from the adolescent and that the involvement of family or peers will not increase friction.

— Allocate sufficient appointment time for the needs of the adolescent. The initial assessment of the young person may take a substantial amount of time.

— The interview needs to be specifically tailored to engage the adolescent. The use of open questions or reassurances such as "many young people I see feel sad' do you feel like that' may be helpful.

— Maintaining contact with followup visits or by telephone is important with the care of adolescents. When the patient fails to attend for a scheduled appointment it may be appropriate to telephone him/her to check on how they are progressing.

Improving the recognition of suicide risk

A key issue in recognising the potential for suicide among young people is the maintenance of a high index of suspicion about the possibility of self harm among young people coupled with a knowledge of which adolescents are at highest risk of making an attempt.

The principal risk factors for suicide have been identified as:

— serious mental illness especially depression, schizophrenia, and personality disorders or substance abuse. Comorbidity with more than one of these conditions further increases the risk

— prior suicide attempt

— antisocial, aggressive or impulsive personality traits

— family history of suicidal behaviour

— disadvantaged socioeconomic and educational background.

In addition a number of other factors can be additional risk factors (or possibly triggers which heighten the risk of suicide among those young adults with any primary risk factors). These additional factors include:

— media coverage of suicide

— intoxication

— recent loss, conflict, humiliation or trouble with authority

— other life stresses.

Risk behaviours

Some experts have stated that certain behaviours may be signs of potential or impending suicide. These behaviours include:

— numerous accidents

— extréme risk taking and dangerous behaviour

— discussing death/morbid themes

— giving away favourite possessions

— organising personal affects and arranging wills

— school problems, disciplinary problems and truancy

— antisocial behaviour

— social isolation and impulsivity

— possessing or buying a weapon or other means of suicide

— belligerent or acting out behaviour

— running away from home.

Questioning for suicide risk

Questioning should be clear and direct and undertaken in a nonjudgemental, deliberate and non-threatening manner. In addition observation of the patient and questioning of their friends and parents are often useful.

Aside from information on the patient's risk of suicide the aim is to gather information on the patient's internal and external support systems. Most experts suggest that the following clear and direct questions are the most appropriate method to determine an adolescent's risk of suicide.

— Have you thought about suicide?

— Have you ever tried to kill yourself before? When there is suicidal ideation the following questions may gauge the strength of the ideation, and the likelihood that it will be carried out. In addition, it may also be prudent to inquire about homicidal thoughts using similar questions

— Have you planned how you will kill yourself?

— What is your plan?

— Do you have the means available?

— Do you have access to a firearm?

— In addition, questioning about the presence of any precipitating stressful event(s) should also be undertaken.

When an attempt has been made it is helpful to question the adolescent about the following aspects of the attempt:

— planning (was there premeditation of the attempt, were possessions given away etc)

— lethality i.e., the circumstances of the attempt especially who was nearby and whether discovery was likely, the knowledge of the person about the dangerousness of the method of suicide and their intention to kill themselves

— history of previous suicidal ideation and/or attempts

— any precipitants for the event.

However, these questions have been exposed to only limited empirical scrutiny. A small cross sectional study was undertaken by Pearce and Martin of 307 high school students in the US. Limitations of the study include its small size, use of a highly selected population and cross sectional design. No inferences can be made about the temporal relationship between answers to the questions and actual behaviour and hence their predictive value cannot be ascertained. In addition the study was not based in a clinical setting and does not evaluate the use of the questions as a screening tool for clinicians.

In relation to the high number of young adults who undertake suicidal behaviours while having evidence of a serious mental illness, an assessment of mental status is also a key component of any assessment of suicide risk. A mental status examination is also indicated, the minimal requirements of which usually include assessment of orientation, state of consciousness, cognitive functioning, contact with reality, logicality of thought processes, and insight and judgement.

A general medical history with attention to recent diagnoses and chronic illness is appropriate, along with a psychosocial history (including information about presenting symptoms, relationships with family and friends, life stresses, substance use, and personality factors) and review of the family history (especially with regard to mental illness) is also indicated. Any family history of mental illness is also important information to gather. Other information may be available from other sources such as friends or family members.

In conclusion, although no proven protocol exists there is a general consensus from expert opinion in the literature that clear direct questioning about risk factors is the most appropriate method to assess the risk of suicide for a patient. While it is recognised that none of the risk factors is entirely predictive at the individual level they do provide a reasonable working guide for clinicians to determine which patients are most at risk.

Screening Tools

A number of psychometric tools have been presented in the literature to screen for suicide risk in adolescent/ child populations. Most of the scales offer a number of questions and seek graded responses that can be totalled to define a composite score that assesses overall suicide risk. The scales vary in their method some probe for underlying risk factors such as suicidal ideation or attempts, others broadly characterise the presence of mental illness especially depression, and finally some assess the young person's philosophical attitude to life and death.

Most of the scales are focused on ideation and do not accurately predict the likelihood of suicidal behaviour for the clinician. In addition, the purpose of the scales has not always been clear, in particular, whether they are intended for research or clinical use, and if intended for clinical use, for what population are they most appropriate.

Few of the scales have satisfactory reliability and validity and few of the scales have been applied to young adults. Finally, most of these tools have only been used in research. Consequently no evaluations exist of a psychometric tool that has been used in actual clinical practice and for which there is adequate evidence about its sensitivity, specificity and predictive value. Lewinsohn et al. therefore reviewed 29 measures of suicide risk applicable to adolescents, and concluded that predictive validity has not been documented for any of them. In the absence of this information there is insufficient evidence to warrant the adoption of any tool.

A major underlying problem with these scales (and any actuarial prediction of suicide risk) is that there is a relatively high base rate of risk factors in the general population compared with the relative rarity of suicide. That is, suicide is a relatively rare event in adolescence, although risk factors such as depression and substance abuse are relatively common. While there may be at any one time a relatively high number of adolescents among the highrisk groups, relatively few will kill themselves.

A related issue is that risk factors for an individual cannot necessarily be generalised to a large population conversely risk factors in a large population do not necessarily apply to a given individual. In the clinical situation, risk assessment is based on the individual, and represents the composite evaluation of all the relevant information about risk factors and it is not confined to a predetermined series of questions. That is, the instrument to assess risk is personalised. Furthermore, it is probable that a considerable amount of information about suicide risk of an individual may be generated from often nonverbal information derived from the interaction of the assessor with the patient. Significantly, no large study has attempted to compare clinical judgement with a score on any assessment instrument.

Another underlying problem related to screening tools was demonstrated in the study by Larzelere et al. This study found that it is clearly unethical to examine the outcome of a group at high-risk of suicide without also providing the group with intensive treatment. These patient groups are the most appropriate for a study of the predictive ability of a clinically administered screening tool, however the predictive power of the scale is then influenced by the treatment that these patients receive.

Considering the relative inability of these screening devices to accurately identify which young people were most at risk of suicide, is not surprising that a previous attempt to introduce screening instruments into the assessment of suicide risk among prison inmates in English and Welsh prisons failed to reduce the number of suicides between 1972-1987.

Accepting that screening devices are relatively ineffective it is not surprising that relatively few clinicians actually use these instruments in their practice, preferring instead to pose direct questions about risk factors. Given that a considerable amount of information is generated by the interaction between the clinician and the patient which cannot easily be placed in a series of scales it is not unexpected that most screening devices have proven to be of limited value. An empirical investigation based in the United States has clearly documented that clinicians primarily use an assessment of the presence (or absence) of known risk factors for suicide as their most important criterion when considering whether to hospitalise a suicidal adolescent. The corollary of this conclusion is that for physicians to continue to be effective gatekeepers they need to be kept up to date with the latest information on the proven risk factors for suicide among adolescents.

Management of Suicidal Young People

A number of steps have been found to be critical in the management of suicidal young people in primary care settingss.

Adeauate training and referral links

It is a preliminary requirement that practitioners are adequately trained to manage suicidal young people and that they also regularly update their skills. In addition the practitioner should be aware of, and have contact with, a number of referral organisations specific to the ongoing health needs of adolescents.

Engage the young person in a therapeutic relationship

Regardless of whether the person will be referred on for more definitive management, or not, it is important to ensure that the young person's initial experiences with a health professional in relation to their mental health illness are conducted in the context of a warm and empathic relationship. It is important for the patient to be listened to and to receive some support from the practitioner in relation to their often very stressful situation. It is also important to provide the young adult with some reassurance that the practitioner will try to assist them.

Make an effective clinical Assessment

An expert opinion article by Press and Khan presents a useful overview of the assessment of a potentially suicidal adolescent. The article describes the evaluation of the patient with the assistance of the mnemonic *Malpractice*. This evaluation should include an assessment of the mental status of the patient, a history of past attempts, a description of the lethality of the attempts, whether the patient has positive or negative plans for the future, description of whether the patient is involved in risk taking behaviours specifically their use of alcohol and drugs, question whether there was any recent conflict or past trauma associated with abuse. Assessment of impulsivity, community supports and the patient's exposure to family or peer suicide complete the assessment plan presented by Press and Khan from information gathered from the patient and their significant friends and family.

Decide if hospitalisation or referral is needed

If suicide risk is high admission is necessary or at least referral to an emergency department of a hospital is indicated. If the patient is not admitted it is usually important to arrange for a review, or at least to consult by telephone, with an appropriate mental health care professional, usually a psychiatrist. Absolute criteria for admission include the need for medical management of an attempt (e.g. administration of N-acetylcysteine for paracetamol poisoning), psychiatric management (e.g. psychosis or persisting suicidal intent) and psychosocial support (e.g. no suitable caregivers available) (Trautman and Shaffer 1989). The practitioner will need to consider committal if he/she considers that suicide risk is high but the young person refuses treatment. Several authors have formulated useful acronyms that describe the risk factors for suicide and which can provide a framework for any decision about admission. Hofmann and Dubovsky describes the use of *Sad persons* to assist the clinician to consider the following risk factors when considering whether to admit a patient:

— risk factor

— sex (male)

— age (youth); the scale was intended for all ages

— depression

— previous attempts

— ethanol (or other substance abuse)

— rational thinking loss

— social supports lacking

— organised plan to commit suicide

— no spouse

— sickness any major medical or psychiatric illness.

Hofmann and Dubovsky emphasises that the tool is only an aide de memoire to consider some of the risk factors for suicide and does not present a definitive checklist, and notes that it is usually prudent to err on the side of caution and admit a patient whenever in any doubt. Similar mnemonics exist for evaluating depression and substance abuse and it is mandatory to consider these diagnoses in patients who are being evaluated for their suicide risk.

Based on this information, referral to hospital for possible inpatient care is indicated in many situations, including the following:

— When the young person represents a serious threat to themselves and/or when they require basic care and support that is unavailable at home or in the community.

— When it is appropriate to temporarily remove the young person from a stressful situation.

— When treatment is unavailable in an outpatient setting or when that treatment is not effective.

— Non-medially qualified primary care providers may always wish to consider referral, particularly if an underlying mental or medical illness is apparent.

Referral should be based on an assessment of the person's suicide risk and an assessment of the person's coping and problem solving abilities, including their ability to abstain from suicide, their ability to express their feelings and use any available support people and finally their willingness to call on therapeutic services.

Rather than considering criteria for admission it may be more appropriate to consider what criteria should be met before a patient is allowed to go home, these criteria include:

1. suicidal intent is not present
2. medically stable
3. patient will return before harming himself if suicidal ideas resurface
4. patient is not intoxicated, delirious, or psychotic
5. firearms have been removed
6. acute crisis has been in some way resolved
7. treatment for an underlying psychiatric illness has been resolved
8. physician believes that the patient will attend treatment
9. social supports have been mobilised.

Provide safety for the young adults

The key points include:

— enlist the assistance of their the family and friends

— remove firearms and means to harm themselves

— arrange close supervision and support from appropriate member of friends/family

— consider negotiating a no suicide contract

— arrange follow-up and provide the young adult, and their support person(s), with a written crisis plan listing additional services (professional and patient based) that are available 24 hrs a day

— follow-up on progress should be maintained by the GP and communication between any health professionals involved in the care of a suicidal patient can be vitally important

— frequent visits will be needed to check on progress, support the patient and coordinate the involvement of other professionals as appropriate.

Appropriate Treatment

Population-based prevention is concerned with decreasing the rate of occurrence of new cases of suicidal behaviour and is directed at the entire population of young people. These interventions therefore seek to alter the non-suicidal person's attitude towards suicide, and involve the early identification and treatment of conditions known to predispose to suicidal behaviour.

Population-based prevention typically involves public health programmes that use the tools of health education, health promotion and health protection. These programmes usually have as their main strategy an attempt to improve mental health amongst adolescents. Most of these programmes have been based in schools and most have the following goals:

— to heighten awareness of suicide

— to promote case finding among peers by presenting descriptions of warning signs and avenues for seeking assistance

— to give staff and students information about mental health resources § to improve adolescents coping ability and focus on maintaining psychological good health.

Role of GP in school-based prevention programmes

School-based prevention programmes are common in the United States, Australia and increasingly in New Zealand. These programmes involve the delivery of general information to students about improving mental wellbeing and the provision of specific information about the development of suicidal behaviour among young people and warning signs to facilitate the identification of potentially suicidal peers. In the literature family physicians have sometimes been involved in either delivering a component of these programmes, acting as a resource for youth or providing for youth a point of referral for any adolescents who have concerns about their own, or their friends' mental health e.g. Committee on Adolescence 1994.

Debate exists about the effectiveness of schoolbased suicide prevention programmes. The school-based programme for its ability to enhance the education and coping skills of young adults, while others have slated them as being well intentioned but misguided, and having a number of deleterious effects on students, such as promoting imitation of suicidal acts. Very few systematic controlled evaluations are available of any school-based programmes, including those that have involved primary care practitioners.

Shaffer et al. and Shaffer et al. provide rare exceptions. Their evaluation concluded that there was some limited evidence of an improved attitude and awareness of suicidal behaviour, or coping techniques, among the students, however most improvement appeared to be among the students who already subscribed to most of the ideals of the programme. Concerns exist that some of the information in the programmes may be inaccurate and that they adopt a universal approach, which ignores the students who are at highest risk of suicidal behaviours.

A number of studies have examined the effect of suicide prevention programmes in schools, which have been principally delivered by school personnel. Some studies have found that suicide programmes increase the sense of hopelessness among students or foster acceptance by students that suicide is a valid solution to problems. Significantly only very few of the studies have assessed the actual effect of the intervention on suicidal behaviour. Zenere and Lazarus used a longitudinal design, and found that the number of reported suicide attempts among pupils in a large school system in the United States reduced after the introduction of a school prevention programme.

Vieland et al. found no difference in the incidence of reported suicide attempts before and after the delivery of a suicide prevention programme in 174 students exposed to the programme compared to 207 controls. The study was set in 4 schools in New York (USA) and followup was undertaken over an 18 month period. Orbach and Bar-Joseph found that pupils exposed to a school-based programme exhibited reduced scores on a scale that indicated their suicide potential compared to controls. By contrast Eggert et al. found that the provision of a schoolbased programme did not improve their suicidal ideation in comparison with a control group. Finally Shaffer et al. found among a small number of students that being exposed to the programme made their suicidal ideation worse. In addition, it is notable that most schoolbased prevention programmes have used a stress model to explain suicidal behaviour among young people, and have therefore ignored the overwhelming evidence emphasising the role of mental illness as an important underlying risk factor.

Surprisingly few studies have evaluated the effect of schoolbased programmes on suicidal behaviour and none have undertaken a longterm assessment of the effectiveness of a programme. A correlational study by Lester found that states in the US with more school-based programmes did not have lower suicide rates. Despite the uncertainty that these programmes are generally effective at reducing suicidal behaviour, some have been reported as being successful at improving mental wellbeing. These programmes have been identified as usually including those that have close links to community based health professionals and those that address a number of goals and utilise a number of strategies.

Kazdin and Shaffer et al. have proposed an alternative approach for schoolbased programmes that is based on targeting the specific needs of high-risk groups and/or the high-risk behaviours of adolescents. Two interventions involved health professionals, Pedro-Carroll and Cowen involved mental health professionals while Pless et al. used primary care nurses.

Office-based preventive health care

The US and Canadian Preventive Services Task-forces have both recommended that adolescents should have one or two consultations with a GP for preventive health care. These consultations were intended to enable the identification and subsequent management of any significant risk factors for ill health. Although the Taskforces did not specifically include the identification of risk factors for suicidal behaviour e.g. substance abuse, depression, these visits have been suggested as an ideal opportunity to undertake this task. Interventions to manage these risk factors could then be either provided or arranged by the primary care practitioner.

Provision of youth health clincs

A number of papers have described the provision of youth health clinics. These clinics have often been set up in schools and a number have been staffed by general practitioners or practice nurses. It has been suggested that youth health clinics based in schools may have an important role in preventing adolescent suicide by improving access to health care for young adults, especially among young people with serious risk factors for suicide (specifically depression or substance abuse). In addition it has been proposed that school health clinics can assist with integrating primary care professionals into school settings and have enabled them to participate in school-based prevention programmes.

Most of published research that has considered school health clinics have been descriptive studies detailing the development of a clinic e.g. McClowry et al. or identifying the type of clients that have attended the facility e.g. Chavasse et al. One study examined the potential of the school-based clinic to identify young adults at risk of suicide, however this study was also only descriptive and relied upon an application of the Suicide Probability Scale to assess the risk of suicide among the attenders.

Some doubt exists about the validity of this scale particularly in relation to its application to community-based groups of adolescents. Consequently, the study was not able to assess the effectiveness of the clinic at accurately identifying which young adults were actually most likely to be at risk.

Although not solely based on young people, considerable interest has been attached to the evaluation of a programme that was primarily aimed at improving GP-based care of mental illness. The quasi-experimental study on the island of Gotland (Sweden) reported that the rate of suicide was reduced after the introduction of training programmes for GPs in the recognition and management of depression. The reduction in suicide rates was accompanied by an improvement in other indicators of quality of care (such as decreased hospital admissions and improved prescribing) and a saving in drug and hospital care costs, which far outweighed the cost of the programme.

However, the effect of the education programme was found to attenuate, such that three years after the project had ended the amount of inpatient care for depressive disorders increased, the suicide rate returned to almost baseline levels and the prescription of psychoactive medication stabilised. Rutz et al. suggested that after two years a significant proportion of the GP workforce in the area had changed and these new practitioners had not been exposed to the programmes. In addition, many of the remaining GPs might have forgotten the information presented to them in previous educational programmes. Some caution must be exercised with the author's conclusions from their evaluation of the Gotland programmes.

The Gotland studies used an essentially retrospective longitudinal, cross sectional study design which is prone to significant methodological deficiencies particularly in relation to its limited ability to determine causality, largely as a result of its inherent inability to adequately eliminate bias or confounding as possible explanations for any associations. The Gotland studies also lacked a control group. Consequently, it is unclear as to what extent the improved outcomes can be reliably attributed to the educational campaign. It has been recognised, for example, that administrative changes in the data may have contributed to the findings or changes in socioeconomic status among the population.

The internet and computer-based tools to privent suicide among yound people

The exhaustive array of information on the Internet coupled with increasing interest and access to computers for many adolescents presents an important potential tool for assisting with suicide prevention among young people. Stoney has described the suicide prevention resources available on the Internet, including those related to web pages, electronic mail and usenet news groups, along with the mailing lists that specifically address suicide among youth.

Apart from providing information, young people can also potentially gain valuable support and contact with their peers, particularly with others who are experiencing similar difficulties. Stoney, however, expresses a number of reservations about the quality of some of the information that is available and the potential for negative or even harmful advice that could be given by participants in electronic discussion groups. Stoney also points out that issues such as whether confidentiality should be respected or how the groups can avoid hoax messages have also not been satisfactorily answered.

Baume et al has also expressed concern that the Internet may present a new forum for the public communication of suicide that may increase the likelihood of imitation events among vulnerable young people. Baume et al. presented two case histories that both suggested that interactive suicide notes on the Internet may have been influential in the suicidal death of two young people. Although no actual research has yet been undertaken on the role of the Internet in relation to suicide imitation or prevention, this medium remains of considerable potential importance for young people who have been shown to be the most frequent group to access cyberspace.

Another novel use of computer based technology directed at young people was presented by Horan. Horan assessed the use of computers to assist young people with the improvement of their selfesteem. Although this study did not assess suicidality and was not based in a clinical setting, it does provide an interesting and innovative example of the application of new technology. The trial was a randomised comparison of 56 young people allocated to receive interactive computer cognitive restructuring (intervention group) or relaxation exercises (control group). After one week, various measurements of selfesteem were significantly higher among the intervention group.

Targeted Treatment

Targeted treatments include those interventions that will reduce the potential for suicide among young adults who have significant risk factors, including those individuals who have already made a suicide attempt and those people who have expressed significant suicidal ideation. Some population-based interventions could also be targeted interventions; for example the restriction of access to the means of suicide.

Two general types of treatment for suicidal behaviour have been described in the literature: psychological or psychosocial treatments, and pharmacological therapies. Often the two modalities are used in combination. Generally, there is very limited evidence about the effectiveness of either of these treatments in relation to preventing suicide among young people. Ideally the effectiveness of an intervention should have been demonstrated by large well-conducted randomised controlled trials, however there is very little of this level of evidence available with regard to the prevention of suicide among adolescents.

Among the few randomised-controlled trials that have been carried out there have been significant limitations associated with the rigour of the research. For example, in one of the few studies that found a positive result for the effectiveness of pharmacological treatment among adolescents to prevent suicide, it is notable that only 96 patients were enrolled in the study and the duration of followup was limited to only 8 weeks. Furthermore, despite the short duration of the trial there was significant attrition from the study, 36 out of 96 patients failed to complete the study.

Prevention of suicide by cognetive behavioual Therapy

Cognitive behavioural therapy (CBT) typically involves multiple components and is based on the theory that some people have learned to interpret events negatively. Typically CBT involves teaching a young person to: monitor their thoughts, evaluate these thoughts and restructure them into helpful, positive ways of thinking. The adolescent is then taught to reinforce these new cognitive patterns and facilitated to devise a pattern of relaxation and participation in pleasurable activities to deal with their stress. Interpersonal issues are also addressed and patients are provided with social skills training.

While several small controlled trials have reported favourable results for the use of CBT among adult suicide attempters e.g. Linehan et al., Salkovskis et al., Blackburn et al., no studies have specifically examined the effectiveness of CBT at reducing suicidal behaviour among adolescents. By contrast, a number of studies have evaluated the use of CBT in the treatment of depression among young people. Generally, these studies have found that CBT was effective at treating depression among young people.

CBT has a number of significant disadvantages. It is associated with a considerable time commitment; initially for professionals to learn the technique and then for both practitioners and patients to undertake the treatment. The treatment would be expensive for adolescents attending a fee-for-service primary care centre. Finally, the rapport established by the therapist, and the relationship between the practitioner and patient, would be very important in determining the outcome of treatment.

A variation of cognitive behavioural therapy, dialectic behavioural therapy (DBT) has been developed for use with patients with borderline personality disorder and has been subjected to one small randomised controlled trial with a favourable result. The therapy is based on a positive and validating attitude to patients with borderline personality disorder and involves a clearly structured treatment programme that includes a clear hierarchy of targets.

DBT utilises a variety of methods (including pharmacotherapy, group counselling and individual psychotherapy) in a treatment that is underpinned by dialectical philosophy that assists the patient to understand their problems and provides them with skill based training to overcome their difficulties. Although this treatment appears promising for a group of patients that can be difficult to engage in therapy, the results of further trials are needed to establish the efficacy of this intervention.

Family Therapy

Family therapy in the treatment of suicidal adolescents is

based on the assumption that the suicidal behaviour of the young person is actually a symptom of familial dysfunction. Treatment therefore is aimed at improving family interaction and communication. Alternative problem solving tools are often also presented to the family unit to enable them to respond more constructively to stressful situations in the future.

Family therapy does not have a single methodology but can involve a number of different approaches. Only one controlled trial was found that evaluated the provision of family therapy in a primary care setting. The trial by Harrington et al. found that family therapy provided by a social worker in a patient's home was ineffective at reducing suicidal ideation among young people (aged 13-16 years).

The trial did not assess the effect of the intervention on actual suicidal behaviour. No other controlled trials have been undertaken on primary care based, family therapy among adolescents at serious risk of suicide behaviour, although it has been noted that a randomised controlled trial is currently underway in the UK.

Family dysfunction has been found to be a risk factor for suicidal behaviours and it seems intuitively rational to assume that treatment of the family could reduce the incidence of suicide in young people, although empirical evidence to support this is awaited.

A randomised controlled trial has been undertaken of family therapy, cognitive behavioural therapy and supportive therapy among adolescents referred to an outpatient unit for treatment of their depression. The study found that cognitive behavioural therapy was the most efficacious treatment for depression while all three treatments were equally effective at reducing scores on a suicide prediction scale. However, the study was small and the evaluation was undertaken after a short period of follow-up, in addition there were significant differences between the study groups at the beginning of the trial which suggested that the randomisation process may have been inadequate.

Family therapy has several disadvantages. The treatment relies upon the ability of the therapist to engage the family and is likely to have limited benefit if some family members were unwilling to participate. Family therapy can be expensive which may be a significant barrier for disadvantaged families.

Group support

Fine et al. in a randomised trial compared the provision of a support group for depressed young people aged 13-17 years with social skill training. The study found that there was no significant difference between the two therapies after 9 months, although initial results favoured group support.

Pychoanalysis

Psychoanalytical treatment involves assisting the young person to act out often unconscious conflict(s) within the therapeutic relationship. No controlled trials have been undertaken of the provision of psychoanalytical treatment. Several reviews have suggested that psychoanalysis is an inappropriate treatment for most adolescents, owing to the need for a long duration of treatment and the intense introspection required for the therapy.

Outpatient-based crisis intervention

Two small studies have considered the outpatient management of adolescents with suicidal behaviour by means of short, crisis orientated therapy which focuses on patient problem solving in relation to the stressful event(s) that may have precipitated the suicide attempt. Crisis therapy emphasises the role of the stressful events and suicidal behaviour as a crucible for change. Proponents suggest that the intense emotions and interest of the patient and his/her family and friends surrounding the suicidal attempt can be harnessed to change the patient's attitude or behaviour along with that of the members of their social milieu in order to improve their wellbeing.

The aim of crisis therapy is to decrease lethality in an individual by decreasing the felt perturbation, that is when the person's unbearable problems or injustices are settled they will reconsider suicide. Unfortunately most research evaluating this approach have included only small, descriptive studies that have lacked both a control group and sufficient size to enable any firm conclusions about the effectiveness of the technique e.g. Gutstein and Rudd, Robinson.

Greenfield et al. found that the provision of a crisis intervention service reduced the rate of subsequent hospitalisations without any other adverse outcomes, although the study could not exclude that some other change in practice behaviour, or case mix, may have accounted for the change. The single randomised trial that has compared outpatient crisis oriented short term treatment with traditional inpatient care has been limited by a number of significant flaws.

Problem solving training per se has not been shown to be effective at preventing suicidal behaviour among adolescents, however, in the crisis situation it is presumed that change can occur.

Pharmacotherapy

Studies of the effect of pharmacotherapy on suicidal behaviour are largely confined to research that has examined the relationship between selective serotonin re-uptake inhibitors (SSRIs) and suicidal behaviour. Given the reports of altered serotonin levels in the brain and CSF of suicide victims there has been considerable hope that SSRI may have a significant effect on suicidal behaviour. In addition, the relative safety of fluoxetine in overdose (especially in comparison with tricyclic antidepressants) has added to the interest in using this medication to treat suicidal adolescents.

However, clinical trials evaluating the efficacy of this medication among either adult or adolescent populations have found mixed results. While some research has found that fluoxetine has failed to reduce the rate of further attempts in a group of depressed adults who have made suicide attempts, another descriptive study by King et al. reported an increase in suicidal behaviour among young people in relation to the use of fluoxetine.

A recent metaanalysis which assessed the effect of fluoxetine on suicidality concluded that neither suicidal behaviour nor ideation were increased by the administration of the SSRI, and although there was a significant reduction in ideation there was no statistically significant effect on suicidal acts and attempts. It is notable that the meta-analysis only included one trial that was solely based on young people. Finally, despite the use of pooled data the meta-analysis probably had inadequate power to assess the impact of the medication on suicide deaths and attempts. Studies that have examined the effectiveness among young people of pharmacotherapy on psychiatric conditions closely associated with suicide

Tricyclic antidepressants (TCAs)

To date, double blind randomised controlled trials of tricyclic antidepressants for adolescents have failed to find any significant benefit over placebo in the treatment of depression even when plasma levels have been monitored. A recent meta-analysis that combined the results of 12 randomised-controlled trials concluded that there was no significant difference between TCAs and placebo in the treatment of adolescent depression. This finding is in marked contrast to the proven efficacy of the medication in the adult population. The discrepancy between adults and adolescents may be due to biological differences between the populations or inadequacies in the design of studies that have assessed the use of the medication in the younger age group.

Many of these patients withdrew because of side effects from the medication. Although no clear benefit has been found with the use of tricyclic medication, several significant adverse effects among adolescents have been recognised with the use of the drug, including cardiotoxic effects and the marked toxicity of the drug in overdose.

Mono- Amne Oxdase Inhibitors (MAOIs)

No randomised-controlled trials have specifically assessed

the effectiveness of MAOIs for the treatment of depression among young people. The potential for this medication to cause serious side effects when used in combination with tyramine-containing foods has limited the use of the medication in young adults.

Selective Serotonin Re-uptake Inhibitors (SSRIS)

Emslie et al. has found in a recent randomised controlled trial involving 96 patients between 6-18 years that fluoxetine (an SSRI) was superior to pla-cebo in the treatment of depression. By contrast an earlier, and smaller trial (n=40), by Simeon et al. (1990) failed to find evidence for the efficacy of fluoxetine in young people aged 13-18 years.

Fluoxetine has been associated with fewer significant side effects than TCAs. Although definitive evidence is not yet available that SSRIs are effective at treating depression in young people (unlike adults where substantial evidence has been accumulated) the medication does appear to be potentially effective.

Bibliography

Adcock, A, Nagy S, Simpson, J., 'Selected risk factors in adolescent suicide attempts', *Adolescence, vol.* 26, no. 104, pp. 817-28, 1991.

Andrews, J, Lewinsohn, P., 'Suicidal attempts among older adolescents-Prevalence and co occurrence with psychiatric disorders', *Journal of the American Academy of Child and Adolescent Psychiatry,* vol. 31. no. 4. ss. 655-62, 1992

Breslau, N, Davis, G, Andreski, P, 'Migraine psychiatnc disorders, and suicide attempts-An epidemiologic study of young adults', *Psychiatry Research,* vol. 37, no.1, pp. 11-23, 1991.

Brown, L. et al, 'Correlates of planning in adolescent suicide attempts', *Journal of the American Academy of Child and Adolescent Psychiatry,* vol. 30, no.1, pp. 95-99, 1991.

Bukstein, O. et al 1993, 'Risk factors for completed suicide among adolescents with a lifetime history of substance abuse-A case-control study', Acta Psychiatrica Scandinavica vol 88 no 6 pp 403-408.

Celotta, B., 'The Aftermath of suicide-Postvention in a school setting', Journal of Mental Health Counseling, vol.17, no. 4, pp. 397-412, 1995.

Cohen, Y., 'Gender identity conflicts in adolescents as motivation for suicide', *Adolescence,* vol. 26, no.,101, pp.19-29, 1991.

Colt, George Howe, *The Enigma of Suicide* N.Y.: Touchstone, 1991

DeSimone, A, Murray, P, Lester, D., 'Alcohol use, self-esteem, depression, and suicidality in high school students', *Adolescence*, vol. 29, no.116, pp. 939-42, 1994.

Eggert, L et al, 'Prevention research program-Reconnecting at-risk youth. Special Issue-Mental health nursing 2000-Issues and challenges', *Issues in Mental Health Nursing*, vol. 15, no. 2, pp. 107-35, 1994.

Ferdinand, R, Verhulst, F., 'The prediction of poor outcome in young adults-Comparison of the Young Adult", *Self-Report, the General Health Questionnaire and the Symptom Checklist'*, Acta Psychiatrica Scandinavica, vol. 89, no. 6, pp. 405-10.

Frankel, B, Kranz, R., Straight talk about teenage suicide, *Facts on File*, New York, reference - 616.8584450835 FRA, 1994.

Garrison, C., et al 'A longitudinal study of suicidal ideation in young adolescents', *Journal of the American Academy of Child & Adolescent Psychiatry*, vol. 30, no. 4, pp. 597-603, 1991

Ho, T., et al 'Characteristics of youth suicide in Hong Kong', *Social Psychiatry and Psychiatric Epidemiology*, vol. 30, no. 3, pp. 107-12, 1995.

Jack, R., *Women and attempted suicide*, Lawrence Erlbaum, Hove, U.K, reference-363.28082 JAC, 1992

Jensen, G., 'Dissociation and suicide in the young', *American Journal of Psychiatry*, vol.149, no.4, pp. 578-9, 1992.

Kosky, R, Goldney, R., 'Youth suicide-A public health problem', *Australian and New Zealand Journal of Psychiatry*, vol. 28, no. 2, pp. 186-187, 1994.

Lukas, C, and Seiden, H., *Silent Grief* N.Y.: Scribner, 1987

Peck, M, Farberow, N, Litman, R., *Youth suicide*, Springer Publ., New York, reference -362.280835 PEC, 1985.

Podnieks, M, Howard, J., "Suicide prevention- Training and awareness-Train the trainer manual", National Youth Foundation, *Suicide Prevention Australia*, Haymarket, N.S.W, reference-616.858445007 POD, 1993.

Robinson, Rita, *Survivors of Suicide* CA: IBS Press, 1989

Index